Collins · do brilliantly !

Includes Tony Buzan's
Mind Maps ®

ExamPractice

GCSE Modern World History

Exam practice at its **best**

■ **Allan Todd**

■ **Series Editor: Jayne de Courcy**

William Collins' dream of knowledge for all began with the publication of his first book in 1819.
A self-educated mill worker, he not only enriched millions of lives, but also founded a flourishing publishing house.
Today, staying true to this spirit, Collins books are packed with inspiration, innovation and practical expertise.
They place you at the centre of a world of possibility and give you exactly what you need to explore it.

Collins. Do more.

Published by Collins
An imprint of HarperCollins*Publishers*
77–85 Fulham Palace Road
Hammersmith
London W6 8JB

Browse the complete Collins catalogue at
www.collinseducation.com

© HarperCollins*Publishers* Limited 2005

First published 2001
This revised edition published 2005

10 9 8 7 6 5 4 3 2 1

ISBN 0 00 719498 6

Allan Todd asserts the moral right to be identified as the author of this work.

British Library Cataloguing in Publication Data
A Catalogue record for this publication is available from the British Library

Edited by Neil Morris
Picture research by Caroline Thompson
Mind Maps artwork by Kathy Baxendale
Production by Katie Butler
Book design by Bob Vickers
Printed and bound by Printing Express, Hong Kong

Acknowledgements
The Author and Publishers are grateful to the following for permission to reproduce questions from past examination papers:
AQA: pp. 29, 39-40, 42 Q1, 50, 51, 66, 81
CCEA: p. 80
Edexcel: pp. 25, 28 Q3, 35-6, 44, 65, 72-3, 82
OCR: pp. 17, 21, 28 Q2, 54-5, 77-8
WJEC: pp. 27, 32, 43, 47, 69-70
Answers to questions from past examination papers are entirely the responsibility of the Author and have been neither provided nor approved by the examining boards.

Photographs
The Publishers would like to thank the following for permission to reproduce photographs (T = Top, C = Centre, B = Bottom, L = Left, R = Right):
AKG London, 56; by permission of the British Library (shelfmark 1856g8), 32B; David Low, Evening Standard / Centre for Study of Cartoons and Caricature, University of Kent, Canterbury, 21TL; 59, Will Dyson, Daily Herald / Centre for Study of Cartoons and Caricature, University of Kent, Canterbury, 20, Bill Partridge, Punch Ltd / Centre for Study of Cartoons and Caricature, University of Kent, Canterbury, 21BR; Leslie Illingworth, Daily Mail / Centre for Study of Cartoons and Caricature, University of Kent, Canterbury, 81; Corbis, 60, 61, 67; Mary Evans Picture Library, 27, 69, 72; The Hulton Getty Picture Collection, 10T, 16T&B, 47, 52, 53C; The Illustrated London News Picture Library, 22C; The Trustees of the Imperial War Museum, London, 15; David King Collection, 30, 32T, 38, 43; Popperfoto, 22B, 23B, 37, 52BR, 74-6; Punch Ltd, 58; Suddeutscher Verlag Bilderdienstt, Munich, 22T, 28, 44; Topham Picturepoint, 10C, 11, 16C, 23C, 24, 45

Every effort has been made to contact the holders of copyright material, but if any have been inadvertently overlooked, the Publishers will be pleased to make the necessary arrangements at the first opportunity.

You might also like to visit:
www.harpercollins.co.uk
The book lover's website

Contents

How this book will help you by Allan Todd

Exam practice – how to answer questions better

This book will help you improve your performance in your Modern World History exam. When you answer exam questions **it is vital that what you write is not only correct – but that it also answers the question**. In other words, to get a high grade in GCSE History you have to do two things: **show what you know and what you can do with what you know**.

Every year, I mark papers where candidates fail to get the grade they are capable of, not because they don't know enough facts, but because they do not deal with the different kinds of questions in the best way. **You will get a high GCSE History grade through a combination of good knowledge, good understanding and good exam technique. It is the last of these that this book will help you improve.**

Each chapter in this book is broken down into four separate elements, aimed at giving you as much guidance and practice as possible:

1 'Key dates to remember'

A book of this size can't include all the historical facts that you will need to do well in your History exam. However, each chapter starts with a 'Key Dates to Remember' section which lists **the most important dates and events that you will need to cover when revising a particular topic.**

2 Exam Question and Student's Answer

I have selected **exam questions from across all the different Exam Boards**. The students' answers to them are typical ones: they show the mistakes candidates frequently make in Modern World History exams.

I explain where the student lost marks, e.g. by not doing what the question asks, or not giving enough detailed historical information to support the answer. I then show you how to gain the extra marks so **that when you meet these sorts of questions in your exam you will know exactly how to answer them and gain full marks.**

4 Questions to try, Answers and Examiner's hints

Each chapter ends with at least one exam question for you to try answering. Don't cheat. Sit down and try to answer each question as if you were in an exam. Try to remember all you've read earlier in the chapter and put it into practice.

Check your answer through and then look at the answer given at the back of the book. These answers are ones that would gain full marks. **The 'What makes this a good answer?' section highlights why marks are gained.** Compare your answer with the answer given and see whether you have written an answer which would gain full marks and, if not, what aspects you need to improve on.

3 'Don't make these mistakes'

This section **highlights the most common mistakes I see every year in students' exam papers**. These include mistakes frequently made by students when reading exam questions, e.g. **describing** an event when the task is to **explain** why it happened. When you're into your last-minute revision, you can quickly read through all these sections to make doubly sure you avoid these mistakes in your exam.

Types of exam questions

Regardless of your Board/specification, your answers will be **level-marked**. This means that, for each question, there will be a mark scheme – normally with two or three levels, but sometimes more. For example, a straightforward question asking you to show what a source tells us about an event, with a maximum mark of 4, might have a mark scheme like this:

Level 1: Simple comprehension, picking out one or two points   1–2 marks

Level 2: Developed comprehension, picking out points, and making an inference/judgement or using some knowledge to explain the content of the source   3–4 marks

The examiner marking your answer then has to decide which level it fits. The decision will be based on **the quality of your answer**, i.e. have

you read the question carefully, done what it has asked and, where appropriate, selected relevant facts from your knowledge? Remember – examiners **don't** award levels on **quantity**. Very often, candidates who focus on the question and don't waste words can reach the top levels, even though writing much less than those who either misread the question or 'waffle'.

You will have to sit **two different papers** for your Modern World History exam: one based mainly on testing your **knowledge** (though there might also be some questions based on sources), and one dealing mainly with **sources** but also requiring you to use your knowledge as well.

This book gives you plenty of practice with the **seven main types of questions** you are likely to meet.

Type of question	How to get top marks	Most common mistakes
1 Recall/describe (or 'What')	These often only need answers of one or two lines, or paragraphs, to give the **main facts** of some historical event, important law, etc.	(a) Vague/unspecific knowledge (b) Spending too long/giving too much information when such questions only carry a few marks
2 Analysis/explanation ('How' or 'Why')	You need to **explain** (not just describe) why something happened or was important; or **how** (or to what extent) **something changed**. These answers need planning, and should give a range of factors/reasons, with **precise knowledge** to support.	(a) Just describing (b) Listing/identifying – but not explaining – one or more factors (i.e. no supporting knowledge) (c) Identifying and explaining one reason only – i.e. a limited or **unbalanced** answer (d) If sources are involved, only dealing with **either** sources **or** own knowledge
3 Judgement or interpretation	You may be asked whether you agree with a statement; the Principal Examiner will be expecting you to comment on the statement, and then to look at other factors – with precise supporting knowledge – to produce a **balanced** answer. You will also need to make a **judgement**; or to suggest that all the factors are linked, so there is no one factor which is most important.	(a) Saying yes/no, but only looking at **one** factor/view (b) Giving a balanced answer by looking at several factors (i.e. yes and no), but not making an **overall judgement** (c) If sources are involved, either failing to deal with these **and** own knowledge; or only considering one or two sources when the question refers to five or six
4 Source comprehension or understanding	As well as pointing out several facts from the source, you will need to make some **general inference or overall summary**, and perhaps give a little own knowledge to help explain the source's information.	(a) Simply copying out a written source, or just describing a cartoon or photo (b) Writing an essay, with lots of knowledge (c) Commenting about the source's nature (e.g. type of source, etc.)

Type of question	How to get top marks	Most common mistakes
5 **Source reliability or utility**	These require you to assess one or more sources for either reliability or usefulness – you will need to consider the content and the nature of the source(s). Such factors should include: type; who wrote/drew/took it; when; typicality; limitations; and especially possible motives/purpose. So you **must** use the important clues in the **provenance/attribution details** (the information about each source) provided for you by the Principal Examiner.	**(a)** Not commenting on all the sources mentioned in the question **(b)** Dealing only with the content – e.g. 'It shows/says...' – and not using the information (provenance/attribution) for each source to comment on their **nature** **(c)** Only dealing with reliability when the question is about **usefulness** **(d)** Simple/general comments – e.g. 'All photographs can be faked, so it is useless' **(e)** Not saying which source is more reliable/useful, if you have been asked to make a choice
6 **Comparison/ cross-referencing of sources**	You must show clearly how the information in one source agrees and does not agree with that of other sources. You must try to look for specific/detailed examples of agreement **and** disagreement.	**(a)** Not using all the sources mentioned in the question **(b)** Just describing each source in turn, with no attempt to **link** them **(c)** Simply making a general comparison – e.g. 'They are all about the Wall Street Crash'
7 **Source sufficiency**	You must assess one or more sources to show to what extent it/they provide enough evidence about a particular topic. To do this, you will have to extract as much information as possible from the sources **and** use your own knowledge to fill in any gaps, and show how their content is correct/sufficient.	**(a)** Not using all the sources mentioned in the question **(b)** Commenting **either** on the content of the source(s) **or** using own knowledge – you must do **both**

Topics required by your Exam Board

This book has 10 chapters which cover the most popular topics of the GCSE Modern World History specifications offered by the main Exam Boards in England and Wales.

The chart below shows you at a glance the coverage provided by this book for the specification you are following:

	AQA	Edexcel	OCR	WJEC
1 The First World War	✓	✓	✗	✗
2 The Peace Treaties	✗	✓	✓	✗
3 Weimar and Nazi Germany, 1918–1945	✓	✓	✓	✓
4 The Russian Revolution	✓	✓	✓	✓
5 Stalin's Russia	✓	✓	✓	✓
6 The USA, 1918–1941	✓	✓	✓	✓
7 International relations, 1918–1939	✓	✓	✓	✓
8 The Second World War	✓	✓	✓	✓
9 Britain, 1900–1945	✓	✓	✓	✓
10 The Cold War	✓	✓	✓	✗

✓ means part of specification ✗ means not part of specification

Why MIND MAPS® will help you

Introduction by TONY BUZAN

Mind Maps really are a shortcut to exam success. They can help you to plan your revision, to organise your work and to remember important information in your exams.

What is a Mind Map?

First of all, a Mind Map is a way of organising your thoughts. Then, because you have created it yourself, and used colours and pictures to make it 'stick' in your brain, it is a way of helping you to remember those thoughts.

A Mind Map is like exercise for your brain. The shapes, colours and pictures on your Mind Map keep your brain active and help you to remember the important facts and ideas.

How do I create a Mind Map?

An example Mind Map for World War I is shown below. This shows you some of the important rules to follow:

- Start with paper, lots of coloured pens, and The Big Idea.
- Turn the paper sideways and write the name of a subject – or the big idea – in the middle of the paper. Add a drawing to help you remember. You don't have to be a great artist: the important thing here is to keep things lively and colourful.
- Now let your imagination get to work! Draw 4 or 5 branches from the central idea for each of the main topics. Write the key word for that topic on the branch, filling up the length of the branch.
- Then you can add smaller branches as you think of how each main topic can break down further. Use only one word for each idea.
- Use a different colour for each main branch and its sub-branches. Colour adds fun and will help you remember.
- Illustrate the branches with small pictures, shapes and colours.
- You can use arrows, underlining or boxes, to link ideas on different branches.

Throughout this book, you will find 'starter' Mind Maps, where we have given you some suggestions to start you off. It's up to you to decide how you are going to complete them. The real value of a Mind Map comes when you create your own.

Not just facts and figures

A Mind Map is about much more than remembering facts, figures, vocabulary, names, dates and places. You can also use them to help plan your essay answers and to remember the best way to answer questions. So why not start a Mind Map with one of the GCSE questions from this book at the centre of the paper? Then add in all the things that make a good answer for that type of question.

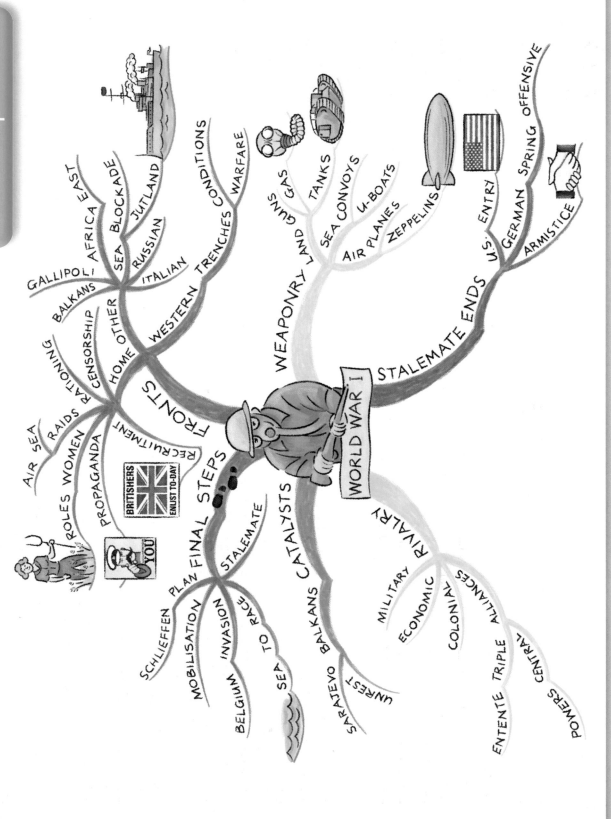

1 The First World War

Key Dates to Remember

Europe, 1914–1918

1914	June	● Assassination of Austrian Archduke in Sarajevo
	August	● Germany declares war on Russia and France, then invades Belgium; Britain declares war on Germany
		● DORA passed by British parliament
	Aug.–Sept.	● Russian defeats at battles of Tannenberg and Masurian Lakes
	September	● Battle of the Marne
	November	● First battle of Ypres; Race to the Sea establishes trench system on Western Front
1915	January	● First Zeppelin raids on Britain (East Anglia)
	March	● Start of the battle of Gallipoli
	April	● Second battle of Ypres; first use of poison gas
	July	● 'Munitions crisis' in Britain
1916	January	● Conscription of single men (18–41) begins in Britain
	February	● Women's Land Army set up in Britain
		● Start of battle of Verdun
	May	● Battle of Jutland
		● Conscription extended to married men
	July	● Battle of the Somme; first use of tanks
1917	April	● Start of British convoy system
		● US joins Triple Entente against Germany
	July	● Third battle of Ypres (Passchendaele)
	November	● Bolshevik Revolution in Russia; Russian army ceases involvement in the war
		● Battle of Cambrai; tanks play an important role
		● Voluntary food rationing begins in Britain
1918	February	● Compulsory rationing introduced
	March	● Start of Germany's Ludendorff (Spring) Offensive
	August	● Start of Allied counter-offensive on Western Front
	November	● The armistice is signed

Exam Question and Student's Answer

Use sources A and B, and your own knowledge, to explain why the Schlieffen Plan had failed by December 1914.   [8 marks]

SOURCE A
A map from a school textbook, published in 1998, showing the extent of the German invasion of France by September 1914.

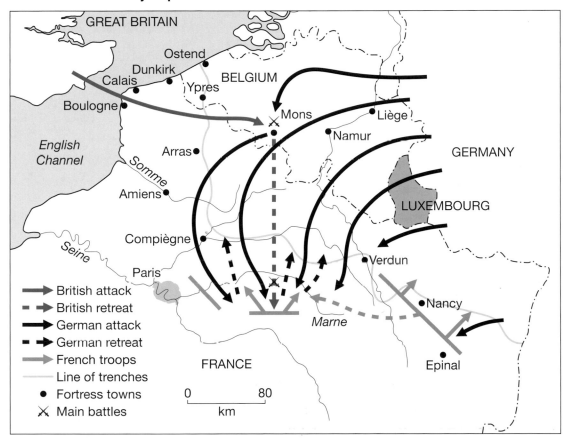

SOURCE B
A photograph of French soldiers being transported to the battle of the Marne in September 1914. Some of the 600 Parisian taxis used can be seen.

1

The German army's Schlieffen Plan did not go according to plan – as Source A shows, they were not able to get behind Paris and cut it off. The Germans had expected the Plan to work, as they needed to defeat France before the Russian army was ready to fight. They had also expected their attack to be rapid, like their earlier defeat of France in the Franco-Prussian War in 1870-71. Once the line of trenches had been dug, after the Race to the Sea – which Source A shows stretched from the North Sea to Switzerland – such a quick victory was impossible. One of the reasons why the trenches had been dug was to avoid the effect of heavy machine guns which killed large numbers of attacking troops. New weapons such as these were possessed by both sides, and were better suited to defence than attack. As a result, the trenches were reinforced and protected by barbed wire – this made rapid advances even more difficult. Before then, everyone had thought the war would be over by Christmas.

Another reason why the Schlieffen Plan failed was that all the sides had large armies that were roughly equal in size, so no country was able to have an advantage.

The main reasons the Plan failed were because of the Belgians and the Russians. The Belgians refused to just let the German army through, and slowed them down by fighting much harder than the Germans had expected. Also, the Russian army had begun mobilising much sooner than the Schlieffen Plan had predicted, and the fighting on the Eastern Front forced the Germans to send over 100,000 troops which should have been used in the attack on France. This is why the Schlieffen Plan failed.

4/8

This answer scores 4 marks because:

► **it is clearly focused on the main requirement of the question**, which is to **explain why** the Schlieffen Plan failed. The student has resisted the temptation to simply write a **detailed description** of the Plan. **If she had done this, she would not have got above Level 1** (see page 6 for an explanation of level marking);

► **it makes use of one source** (A) to support the comments made ('as Source A shows, they were not able to get behind Paris and cut it off'), and **extracts information from that source** (that the line of trenches 'stretched from the North Sea to Switzerland');

► **it adds to the source by using some of the student's own knowledge to explain why** the Plan failed: the Race to the Sea, Belgian resistance, new weapons, size of opposing armies and the need to divert troops to the Eastern Front;

► **it shows good general understanding** of the Schlieffen Plan and its main purpose (the need to 'defeat France before the Russian army was ready to fight').

To score full marks, you also need to:

► **use BOTH of the sources** to explain the failure of the Plan – the **attribution/ provenance** details provided for Source B make a clear reference to the important battle of the Marne, when the Allies counter-attacked;

► **use more 'own knowledge'.** As well as explaining what happened at the battle of the Marne, your answer could refer to **the first battle of Ypres in November 1914; Britain declaring war and sending the BEF** (which forced the German army to go east of Paris, not west as in the original Plan); **the exhaustion of the German troops** after three weeks of fighting and rapid advance (long supply lines meant German soldiers often had insufficient food).

DON'T MAKE THESE MISTAKES ...

✗ Always read the words of the question carefully. **Don't just describe if you have been asked to explain**.

✗ When adding 'own knowledge', make sure you **use relevant facts**. Don't be satisfied with just one piece of extra information – try to **think of several aspects** to include in your answer.

✗ If a question asks you to use **two or more sources**, make sure you **say something about ALL of them** – even if it is only a brief comment. If you don't, you will lose marks.

✗ If a question **asks you to use your own knowledge**, as well as the sources, make sure you do **both**. Many good candidates limit themselves to scoring half marks because they only use the sources or their own knowledge.

✗ **NEVER ignore the attribution/provenance details of the sources.** These are provided to help you write a top-level answer.

Questions to try

Question 1   EXAMINER'S HINTS

✔ Remember to look carefully at the **marks available** for each question.
These are a rough indication of how much you should write.

✔ Look carefully at the **wording of a question**. A 'why' question expects you to
explain something; if you only describe, you will score a low mark,
even if your knowledge is very detailed and accurate.

(a) What was meant by the term 'Pals Regiment'?

[2 marks]

(b) What were the key features of the Defence of the Realm Act (DORA) of 1914?

[5 marks]

(c) Why was conscription introduced by the British government in 1916?

[8 marks]

Question 2   EXAMINER'S HINT

✔ Remember to use **all the sources** referred to AND your **own knowledge**.
If you only do one of these, you will limit yourself to half marks at most.

Do Sources A, B and C provide enough information about the role played by British women
during the First World War?
Use all three sources, and your own knowledge, to explain your answer.   [10 marks]

SOURCE A
**A photograph of a
woman munitions
worker during the
First World War.**

SOURCE B
An extract from the *Forget-Me-Not* magazine, published in Britain in June 1915.

For nearly three years I have had a sweetheart whom I love deeply. He is 25 and I 18. He is eligible for the army but has never offered ... Most of my girlfriends' sweethearts have gone and I feel horrid when I meet them with my boy: the humiliation is dreadful ... shall I give him up or not?

SOURCE C
A recruiting poster, issued by the British government during the First World War, to persuade women to join the Voluntary Aid Detachment (VAD).

2 The Peace Treaties

Key Dates to Remember

1918–1924

| 1918 | January | • Wilson's Fourteen Points |
| | November | • Armistice is signed by a new German government |

1919	January	• The 'Big Three' meet in Paris for the start of the Peace Conferences
		• The Spartacist Rising in Germany
	June	• Treaty of Versailles signed by Germany
	September	• Treaty of St Germain signed by Austria
	November	• Treaty of Neuilly signed by Bulgaria

1920	January	• League of Nations begins its work
	March	• Treaty of Trianon signed by Hungary
		• Treaty of Sevres signed by Turkey

| 1921 | | • Reparations Committee fix Germany's payment of compensation at £6,600 million |

| 1923 | January | • France and Belgium occupy the Ruhr (because of Germany's non-payment of the second reparations instalment) |
| | | • Treaty of Lausanne signed with Turkey, after the Treaty of Sevres was rejected by the new nationalist government |

| 1924 | April | • Dawes Plan drawn up to help Germany with the reparations payments |

Exam Questions and Students' Answers

1 Explain why the Allies punished Germany in the Treaty of Versailles.   [6 marks]

> The Allies punished Germany by the Treaty of Versailles because they blamed Germany for starting the First World War. So they thought it was fair to make Germany pay for the damage. Also, France in particular wanted to weaken Germany.
>
> **3/6**

This answer scores half marks because:

► it shows a **good general understanding** of the historical background to the Treaty of Versailles;

► it **explains rather than simply describing**;

► it clearly **identifies three reasons** why the Allies punished Germany.

To score full marks, you also need to:

► **give plenty of historical facts to explain each** of the reasons. Your answer needs to explain **why**:

i)   **the Allies believed Germany was to blame** (e.g. by encouraging Austria to risk a conflict with Russia over Serbia; invading Belgium);

ii) **France in particular wished to keep Germany weak** (i.e. to prevent Germany ever being strong enough, economically and militarily, to start another war);

iii) **Britain and especially France needed money to pay for the cost of the war** (both had huge debts to the US, and there had been tremendous destruction of factories, transport and land in France).

2 'The most important reason why Germany hated the Treaty of Versailles was the loss of territory.'
Do you agree with this statement? Explain your answer.   [10 marks]

> I agree that the loss of territory was an important reason why Germany hated the Treaty of Versailles, but I do not agree that it was the most important reason.
>
>   Many Germans hated the Treaty because by taking away all its colonies and making it give up land in Europe as well

(e.g. Alsace-Lorraine), it made Germany weaker and poorer, and most Germans felt humiliated. In particular, most Germans were angry at having to give Poland the Polish Corridor (West Prussia and Posen) as this split East Prussia from the rest of Germany.

However, the War Guilt Clause (Article 231) was really more important, because Germany was not totally to blame for the war, but this clause was forced on Germany and was then used by the Allies to justify punishing Germany in many ways. In particular, it led to Germany being forced to pay reparations or compensation. This was finally decided in 1921, and it was very high – £6,600 million. This caused problems for the German economy (such as hyper-inflation) and most Germans hated the War Guilt Clause and having to pay reparations.

$^8/_{10}$

2 ▸ **This answer scores 8 marks out of a possible 10 because:**

▸ it does more than just list some reasons – the student tries to **explain why** the various reasons given are important;

▸ it does not simply agree or disagree with the question's statement, but **compares a couple of reasons**, and then **makes a judgement/decision** ('the War Guilt Clause was really more important');

▸ it makes **good use of own knowledge** to support the points made (e.g. the land losses in Europe; the loss of colonies abroad; specific information about the War Guilt Clause).

To score full marks, you also need to:

▸ consider a **wider range of possible reasons** (for instance, you should discuss **the military restrictions** of the Treaty: the German army was limited to only 100,000; it was not allowed to have an airforce and its navy was to be severely reduced, with a total ban on submarines). You also need to mention the ban on union – or *Anschluss* – with Austria.

▸ try to achieve **a more balanced answer**. Your answer could be structured to show that **all the various reasons were linked and equally hated**. Most Germans hated the Treaty as a whole for the various ways in which it humiliated German pride and undermined national identity, which had already been badly affected by the fact that Germany had been defeated.

DON'T MAKE THESE MISTAKES ...

✗ When answering 'why' questions, **don't just list a number** of reasons, or be satisfied with giving one reason. **Expand on the reasons**, by giving **facts** that **explain and show why they were important.**

✗ If a question offers a historical interpretation or statement based on one factor, **never limit yourself to comments on that factor alone.** You must deal with the given one, and then **try to write about several other factors**, in order to **produce a BALANCED answer.**

✗ If a question asks you to agree/disagree with a particular statement or interpretation, make sure you do **make a final judgement/decision.** If you don't, you will not reach the top level.

Mind Map

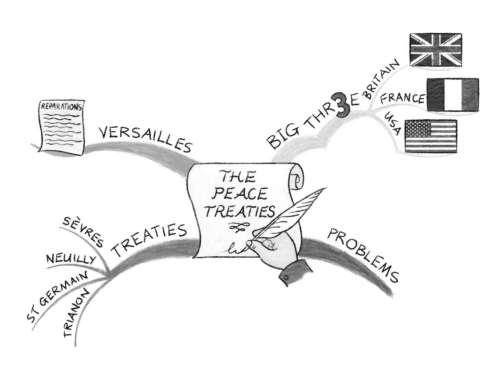

Questions to try

Study Source A. What view of the Treaty of Versailles is suggested by the cartoonist? Give reasons for your answer.   [4 marks]

SOURCE A
A cartoon, produced in 1919 by the British artist W. Dyson, shortly after the Treaty of Versailles was signed.

Question 2 — EXAMINER'S HINTS

✔ Look closely at the **wording** of the question – the words used are carefully selected clues from the Principal Examiner to you. A 'how far' question means that the Principal Examiner will be expecting you to find agreements **and** disagreements.

✔ Make sure you refer to **both** cartoons. If you only deal with one, you will not be comparing.

✔ Make sure you support any comments by picking out details from the cartoons.

Study Sources B and C. How far do these cartoons agree?
Explain your answer, using details of the cartoons.

[7 marks]

Lloyd George: "Perhaps it would pull better if we let it touch earth."

SOURCE B
A cartoon from a British newspaper, January 1921. It shows Briand holding the horse's rein while Lloyd George looks on.

Germany: "Help! Help! I drown! Throw me a lifebelt!"

Lloyd George and Briand: "Try standing on your own feet."

SOURCE C
A cartoon from a British magazine, 1921. It shows Germany kneeling in the water, while Lloyd George and Briand look on.

3 Weimar and Nazi Germany, 1918–1945

Key Dates to Remember

Germany, 1918–1945

1918	November	• Abdication of Kaiser • New provisional government under Ebert and the SPD • Armistice signed
1919	January	• Spartacist Revolt – crushed by the army and the Freikorps
	April	• Revolution in Bavaria
	June	• Treaty of Versailles
	August	• New constitution for Weimar Republic
	September	• Hitler joins Drexler's DAP
1920	February	• DAP becomes the Nazi Party; 25 Point Programme drawn up
	March	• Kapp's Putsch • Red Rising in the Ruhr
1921	January	• Reparations Committee decides Germany has to pay £6,600 million
	July	• Hitler replaces Drexler as leader of the Nazi Party
	August	• SA formed
1923	January	• French occupation of the Ruhr
	July	• Hyper-inflation
	September	• New German government under Stresemann begins stabilisation
	November	• Munich (Beer Hall) Putsch
1924	August	• Dawes Plan
	December	• Mein Kampf ('My Struggle') written by Hitler while in prison • Nazi Party (banned at the beginning of the year) in a state of disorganisation
1925	February	• Hitler reforms the Nazi Party and begins its reorganisation • SS formed
	October	• Locarno Pact

1926	September	● Germany allowed to join League of Nations
1928	August	● Kellogg-Briand Pact
1929	June October	● Young Plan; death of Stresemann ● Wall Street Crash and start of the Great Depression
1930	September	● Nazis win 107 seats in Reichstag elections
1932	April July November	● Presidential elections – 13 million votes for Hitler, 19 million for Hindenburg ● Nazis become largest party in Reichstag after elections ● Nazis lose some seats in new Reichstag elections
1933	January February March April May July	● Hindenburg persuaded by von Papen to appoint Hitler as Chancellor ● Reichstag Fire – Communist Party banned ● Enabling Act passed – end of the Weimar Republic, start of the Third Reich ● Jewish people banned from the civil service, education and broadcasting; boycott of Jewish businesses ● Trade unions banned; replaced by German Labour Front ● All opposition parties banned
1934	June August	● Night of the Long Knives – murder of SA leaders ● Death of Hindenburg; Hitler appointed as Führer
1935	March November	● Re-armament and conscription ● Nuremberg Laws against Jewish people
1937	August	● Four-Year Plan
1938	November	● *Kristallnacht* ('The Night of Broken Glass')
1939	July September	● Membership of Nazi Youth movements made compulsory ● Start of the Second World War
1942	January	● Start of the Final Solution
1945	April	● Hitler commits suicide; end of the Third Reich

Exam Questions and Students' Answers

Study Sources A, B and C carefully and then answer the questions below.

SOURCE A
From *Völkischer Beobachter*, the official Nazi newspaper, March 1933.

> *The first concentration camp will open in the next few days, to hold 5,000 prisoners. All Communists and Social Democrats who endanger state security will be imprisoned. The police and the Ministry of Interior are convinced that they are acting in the national interest and that these measures will have a distinct effect upon the whole nation.*

SOURCE B
A photograph showing an SA man arresting suspected Communists, 1933.

SOURCE C
From the law passed in July 1933, which ended the existence of opposition parties in Germany.

> *Article 1:* *The National Socialist German Workers' Party shall be the only party in Germany.*
>
> *Article 2:* *Anyone who organises another political party shall be imprisoned and will serve between six months and three years.*

1 Does Source C support the evidence of Sources A and B? Explain your answer.

[4 marks]

1 I think Source C does support Sources A and B, because in Source A it says that members of the Communist and Social Democrat Parties will be imprisoned and Source C says this will happen in Article 2. Also, Article I in Source C states that the Nazi Party will be the only party in Germany – this means that all other political parties will be illegal, and this agrees with what Source A says.

Source B shows suspected Communists being arrested by the SA, so this supports Source C which says in Article 2 that anyone who organise.s another political party will be imprisoned.

³/₄

This answer scores 3 marks because:

► it makes an attempt **to show how both the sources support Source C;**

► it makes **quite detailed comments on how Source C supports Source A.**

To score full marks, you also need to:

► **make much more detailed reference to Source B** (e.g. the attributions/ provenances of both Sources B and C

show they are from the same year [1933] and Source B refers to the SA, which was an important part of the Nazi Party);

► **try to find some ways in which Source C *does not* fully support the other two sources,** as well as how it does (e.g. Source C refers to an official law, but in Source B the SA are shown doing the arresting, rather than the police).

2 Why did Hitler wish to remove his political opponents? Use Sources A, B and C, and your own knowledge, to explain your answer.

[6 marks]

2 Hitler wanted to remove his political opponents so he could turn Germany into a Nazi dictatorship. If there were no political opponents in the Reichstag, Hitler could

pass any law he liked. He could then give powers to the SA and SS to arrest and get rid of all opponents, like in Source B. With all opponents in concentration camps, as threatened in Source A – or dead – no-one could stop him from carrying out his controversial plans and policies, such as the genocide of all Jewish people living in Nazi-controlled Europe.

3/6

2   **This answer scores half marks because:**

- ▶ it shows **quite good general understanding** of Hitler's plans to set up a dictatorship;

- ▶ **it uses two sources** (A and B) to support a comment;

- ▶ **it shows some own knowledge:** the references made to the Reichstag, the SS and the extermination of Jewish people are not mentioned in the sources;

- ▶ **it gives a clear explanation** ('...so he could turn Germany into a Nazi dictatorship'), and has thus avoided the mistake of simply describing how he removed political opponents.

To score full marks, you also need to:

- ▶ use *all three sources* **to support comments and own knowledge.** Your comments don't necessarily have to be long (e.g. 'Source C shows how quickly Hitler moved, as six months after becoming Chancellor he had outlawed all other parties.');

- ▶ **use much more precise own knowledge** – to add to what the sources show and so give a wider range of reasons. For example, both Source A and Source B refer to the Communists, so your answer could include evidence of the **growth of the KPD** in the 1930s and the **fear of communism.**

DON'T MAKE THESE MISTAKES ...

- ✗ If a question asks you to use all the sources, **make sure you do refer to all the ones mentioned in the question** – even if some of your comments are brief. If you don't, you will lose marks.

- ✗ If a question says 'Why' then **don't just describe**, as this will only get you into the lowest level of marks. **You must try to use your knowledge to explain**.

- ✗ If a source question also asks you to use your own knowledge, **then make sure you do add a reasonable amount of precise and relevant information of your own**.

Questions to try

Question 1	EXAMINER'S HINTS

✔ The question asks you about **the effects of the hyper-inflation of 1923** – as there is no mention of another date, there is no need to say anything much about what happened after 1923.

✔ To score high marks, make sure you **write about more than just one or two effects**.

This question is about the Weimar Republic 1919–1933.

INFORMATION

This poster shows a figure representing the Weimar Republic in 1924 pulling Germany away from the dark years of 1918.

Zur Reichstagswahl am 4. Mai 1924.

What impact did the hyper-inflation of 1923 have on Germany?

[4 marks]

Question 2   EXAMINER'S HINTS

✔ As this is a 'why' question, don't just give a general description of developments in Germany in the 1920s – you must **try to explain** the Nazis' lack of success.

✔ This question carries 6 marks, so make sure you **give several different reasons**.

Why did the Nazis have little political success before 1930?

[6 marks]

Question 3   EXAMINER'S HINTS

✔ Make sure you comment on **both** sources.

✔ As well as dealing with the content of the sources, **make sure you say something about the provenance/attribution information provided for each of the two sources.**

✔ Don't forget to **include words such as 'use' and 'useful'** in your answer.

Study Sources A and B. How useful are these two sources as evidence about the activities of the Stormtroopers (SA) in the years 1933 and 1934?

[8 marks]

SOURCE A
A photograph of Nazi Stormtroopers occupying trade union offices in Munich, in 1933.

SOURCE B
Extract from Hitler's speech to the Reichstag, 13 July 1934, explaining the Night of the Long Knives.

After the month of May, there could be no futher doubt that the Chief-of-Staff of the Stormtroopers (SA), Ernst Röhm, was busy with ambitious schemes which, if carried out, could only lead to the most violent disturbances. The preparations for this revolt were extensive. Only ruthless and bloody intervention could prevent the revolution from spreading.

Question 4

EXAMINER'S HINTS

✔ This is the highest-scoring question you will meet in a History exam, so the Principal Examiner will be expecting you to write an essay. You will therefore need to **write about a wide range of factors**.

✔ **Make sure you do more than just describe the growth of the Nazi Party** in the period 1929 to 1933.

Study the sources below and then answer the question which follows.
Explain how Hitler and the Nazis increased their support in Germany in the period 1929 to Hitler becoming Chancellor in January 1933.   [15 marks]

SOURCE C From a historian writing in 1990.

> In **Mein Kampf**, written in 1924, Hitler put forward ideas that Germany would be great again. Germany would be united and strong under the control of the Führer, and it would control Europe.

SOURCE D From a historian writing in 1992.

> The elections of March 1933 had not given the Nazis a majority in the Reichstag, so Hitler introduced the Enabling Law. This would allow him to make laws for the next four years without having to ask the Reichstag for approval. He now had the power to destroy all opposition.

SOURCE E
Cartoon from an American newspaper published in 1936. Hitler is saying: 'In these three years I have restored honour and freedom to the German people.'

SOURCE F
Numbers of unemployed in Germany between 1933 and 1939.

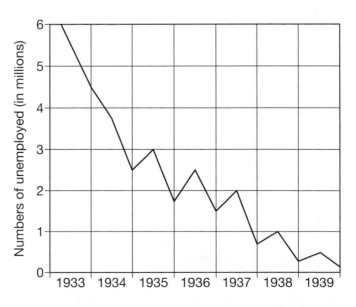

4 The Russian Revolution

Key Dates to Remember

Russia, 1917–1924

1917

March	●	Demonstrations and strikes lead to March Revolution
April	●	Lenin returns to Russia – and issues his 'April Theses'
May	●	Trotsky returns, and applies to join the Bolsheviks
July	●	The 'July Days'; Prime Minister Kerensky bans the Bolshevik Party
September	●	Kornilov's attempted coup prevented by the Bolsheviks' Red Guards
October	●	Lenin persuades the Bolsheviks to plan the overthrow of Kerensky
November	●	Trotsky organises the November Revolution, carried out by the Red Guards

● The All-Russian Congress of Soviets elects a new Bolshevik government (*Sovnarkom*) – Lenin is Chairman (prime minister)

December ● The Left Social Revolutionaries form a coalition with the Bolsheviks

1918

January	●	Bolsheviks close down the newly-elected Constituent Assembly
March	●	Treaty of Brest-Litovsk with Germany. Left SRs leave the coalition government and begin to oppose the Bolsheviks
	●	Trotsky becomes Commissar for War, and the Red Army is formed
May	●	The Civil War between Reds and Whites begins
June	●	War Communism begins
December	●	Foreign armies intervene to help the Whites

1920	March	● Poland invades Russia
	November	● The last major White army is defeated
		● Peace negotiations begin with Poland
1921	March	● Kronstadt Rebellion
		● New Economic Policy ends War Communism; Lenin persuades the Bolsheviks to agree to a temporary ban on factions and opposition parties
1922	May	● Lenin suffers his first stroke
1924	January	● Lenin dies

Mind Map

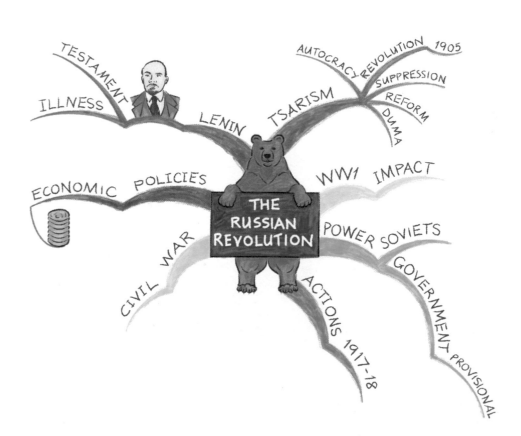

Exam Questions and Students' Answers

Lenin's final years, 1921–1924
Study carefully the sources below and answer the questions which follow.

SOURCE A
A photograph of peasants taken in 1921.

(a) What does Source A tell us about conditions in Russia in 1921?
[2 marks]

The peasants look poor and don't have good clothes. Source A shows them standing around some animal ribs which don't have much meat on them.

½

SOURCE B
A White Russian poster about the Bolsheviks' agricultural policy during the Civil War.

(b) What information does Source B give about Bolshevik agricultural policy during the Civil War?
[3 marks]

Source B shows Red Army soldiers arresting a peasant and taking away sacks of corn. It also shows a soldier killing a goose or chicken.

⅓

SOURCE C
Extract from the demands of the Kronstadt sailors, March 1921.

Because the present Soviets do not express the will of the workers and peasants, new elections should be held. Freedom of speech and press to be granted to workers and peasants. Also freedom of assembly and of trade unions and peasants' associations. All political prisoners belonging to Socialist parties to be set free.

(c) According to Source C, what caused the revolt at Kronstadt?   [4 marks]

Source C shows that the revolt happened because the Soviets did not express the will of the workers and peasants, so they wanted new elections. They also wanted freedom of speech and the press, and of assembly, trade unions and peasants' associations. They also wanted all Socialist political prisoners to be freed.

2/4

These answers score low marks because:

► they **just paraphrase what the sources show or say and don't add own knowledge to explain the sources.**

► In question (a), **you need to link the signs of the peasants' poverty and hunger to the famine** that hit many parts of Russia in 1921.

► In question (b), **you need to use your own knowledge to explain that these actions were typical of the grain requisitions under War Communism,** which the Bolshevik government ordered during the Civil War, in order to feed the Red Army and the factory workers in the towns.

► In question (c), **you need to make a general summary of the information in the source** (e.g. 'the source shows that the Kronstadt sailors were demanding greater democracy/more freedom').

► You also need to **use your own knowledge** to link these sentences to how the Civil War had led to the Bolsheviks arresting the leaders of other parties, closing down opposition newspapers and ignoring the Soviets – and how these developments had disappointed/angered many people.

SOURCE D
Leonid Orlov, a Bolshevik supporter, in his memoirs of 1987, recalling the introduction of the New Economic Policy (NEP)

There wasn't a scrap of food in the country. We were down to a quarter of a pound (114g) of bread per person. Then suddenly they announced the NEP. Cafés started opening, restaurants too. Factories went back into private hands. It was capitalism. In my eyes what was happening was the very thing I'd struggled against.

(d) How useful is this source to a historian studying the New Economic Policy?
   Explain your answer using the source and your own knowledge.   [5 marks]

d

Source D is quite useful to a historian studying the New Economic Policy because it gives useful facts about the poor conditions in Russia before 1921 and so shows why Lenin introduced it in 1921.

   Before then, Lenin had used War Communism to run the Russian economy during the Civil War. This had involved taking grain from the peasants to feed the Red Army and the workers in the towns. But the peasants didn't like this, and began to grow less food. This is shown in the source where it talks about how people only had a quarter of a pound of bread a day. When the Civil War ended in 1920, Lenin kept War Communism going but then decided to introduce the NEP in 1921 in order to get the economy going again. This source is also useful because it shows how the NEP involved allowing factories (which had been nationalised under War Communism) to be owned by capitalists again. It also shows how some Bolsheviks didn't like the NEP.   ⁴/₅

d

This answer scores over half marks because:

► it doesn't just describe/paraphrase the information in the source. Instead, **the information is used to explain or illustrate a point.** For example, the daily ration of bread (a quarter of a pound/114g) is linked to the peasants' reaction (growing less food) to the requisitioning of grain under War Communism.

► **it adds from own knowledge to explain what the source is about.**

To score full marks, you also need to:

► **comment on the provenance/attribution details.** For example, these tell us that the source was from memoirs written over 60 years after the events, so there might be memory problems; and that the writer was a Bolshevik who was against the NEP, so he might have exaggerated because of bias. Both these aspects might make the source less useful.

DON'T MAKE THESE MISTAKES ...

✗ Don't just paraphrase what is provided by a source. This will only get you half marks at most. You should always **try to make some general/overall comment and use some own knowledge to explain the historical background.**

✗ **Don't ignore the provenance/attribution information provided about a source when answering 'usefulness' questions.** As well as commenting on the content of the source(s), and adding some own knowledge to show if the information is accurate, you will need to **write about possible problems of reliability** (when/why was it written/taken? who produced it?)

Questions to try

Question 1 | EXAMINER'S HINTS

✔ This question asks you to **explain** the problems faced by the Bolshevik government in November 1917. **If you only list – or even describe in great detail – the problems, you will only score half marks at most.**

✔ Try to **deal with at least two or three separate problems.** If you only write about one, you will not score high marks.

Explain the problems faced by the Bolsheviks when they came to power in November 1917.

[6 marks]

Question 2 | EXAMINER'S HINTS

✔ This question asks you to explain **to what extent you agree or disagree** with one explanation of why the Tsar fell from power in March 1917. Somewhere in your answer **you will need to say whether you agree/disagree** – as well as writing about several other possible explanations.

✔ Don't forget to **make use of the sources AND your own knowledge.**

'Russia's defeats in the First World War were the main reason for the fall of the Tsar in March 1917.' Use the sources, and your own knowledge, to explain whether you agree with this view.

[12 marks]

SOURCE A
Part of a letter sent home by an officer in the Russian army in late 1918.

At the start of the war we were short of guns and supplies. Some soldiers did not even have a rifle to use against the enemy. We were humiliated by defeat at the battle of Tannenberg. Now the men are splendid. There are plenty of guns and ammunition and yet things are getting worse. The strategies of the generals are brainless. We are ready to die for Russia, but not because a general says so.

SOURCE B
Table showing production in Russia, 1915–16.

Managed to increase the production of...

1915–16

1	**Rifles**	up by 200%
2	**Machine Guns**	up by 300%
3	**Artillery**	up by 400%
4	**Petrol**	up by 12%
5	**Coal**	up by 20% (despite loss of Polish coalfields)

But failed to produce enough...

CEREALS	down by 30%

SOURCE C
From a modern history textbook published in 1979.

Despite all the losses, at the start of 1917 Russia looked strong enough to fight on. The war economy was going full blast. The Russian generals were confident. They had more men, more guns and more ammunition than the enemy. They felt that one great attack on Germany and Russia would recapture the losses of the first two years of the war.

This is a hooligan movement. Young people run about and shout that there is no bread, simply to create excitement. Workers also run around preventing others from working. If the weather was very cold they would probably stay at home. All this will pass and become calm, if only the Duma will behave itself.

SOURCE D
A letter from Tsarina Alexandra to Tsar Nicholas, written on 26 February 1917, about the discontent in Petrograd.

SOURCE E
Photograph of workers protesting in Petrograd during the last week of February 1917. The banner reads 'Militia of the Soviet and Workers' Deputies'.

SOURCE F
From a history textbook about Russia published in 1996.

The overthrow of the Tsar happened more by chance than by any great plan. Some historians even argue that the February Revolution was sparked off by the weather. The first months of 1917 were much colder than usual – temperatures averaged minus 12 degrees Celsius. This extreme cold, on top of food and fuel shortages due to the war, was too much.

Key Dates to Remember

Stalin and Russia, 1922–1939

1922

April	● Stalin becomes General Secretary of the Communist Party
May	● Lenin suffers his first stroke
December	● Zinoviev, Kamenev and Stalin form an alliance against Trotsky
	● Lenin writes his Testament

1924

January	● Lenin dies
April	● 'Socialism in One Country' v 'Permanent Revolution' debate
May	● Zinoviev and Kamenev persuade the Central Committee not to dismiss Stalin as recommended by Lenin in the Postscript to his Testament, and to keep Lenin's views secret. Zinoviev, Kamenev and Stalin (the Triumvirate) begin their campaign to prevent Trotsky becoming the next leader
December	● Stalin joins with Bukharin and the Right in face of growing opposition from Zinoviev and Kamenev

1926

July	● United Opposition formed between Trotsky, Zinoviev and Kamenev

1927

November	● Stalin defeats the United Opposition; Trotsky and Zinoviev are expelled from the Communist Party, while Kamenev loses his seat on the Central Committee

1928

July	● Stalin begins to fall out with Bukharin and the Right over agricultural policy; Bukharin persuades the Central Committee to slow down collectivisation
August	● Bukharin tries to form an alliance with Trotsky to restore Party democracy
October	● Start of the First Five-Year Plan (drawn up by Gosplan)

1929

January	● Trotsky exiled from the Soviet Union
April	● Bukharin defeated over collectivisation of agriculture
November	● Bukharin removed from government and Party positions
December	● Stalin calls for the kulaks to be 'liquidated as a class'

1930	January	●	Start of mass forced collectivisation
1933	January	●	Start of Second Five-Year Plan
1934	December	●	Assassination of Kirov
1935	August	●	Start of 'Stakhanovite' movement to increase industrial output
1936	August	●	Start of First Show Trial; the Great Purge begins
	December	●	Stalin's Constitution introduced
1937	January	●	Second Show Trial
	February	●	Bukharin expelled from the Communist Party
	May	●	Purge of the Red Army begins
1938	January	●	Start of Third Five-Year Plan
	March	●	Third Show Trial
1939	March	●	End of the Great Purge

Mind Map

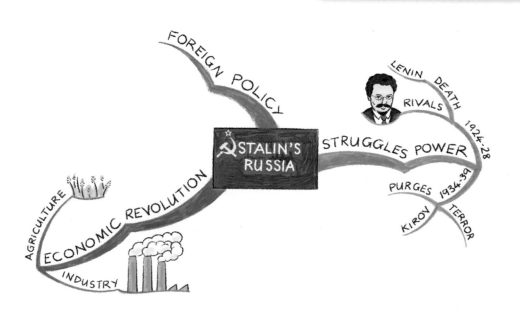

Exam Questions and Students' Answers

Study the sources below and then answer the questions which follow.

SOURCE A
From Lenin's
Political Testament
written in 1923.

> *Stalin has enormous power in his hands as General Secretary. I propose to comrades to find a way to remove Stalin.*

SOURCE B
From a speech by
Stalin in 1931.

> *The history of old Russia has consisted in being beaten again and again because of our backwardness. It is our duty to the working class to increase the pace of production. We are 50–100 years behind the advanced countries. We must make up this gap in ten years. Either we do it or they crush us.*

(a) Study Source A. Use your own knowledge to explain why Stalin was able to succeed Lenin despite the warning given by Lenin in the source.　　　　　　[4 marks]

Stalin was able to succeed Lenin despite Lenin's warning because of his position as General Secretary of the Communist Party of the Soviet Union. He had first been given this job in 1922. It was mainly a fairly boring job, dealing with routine administrative matters – because it was so boring and apparently unimportant, none of the leading Communists wanted the job and thought that it didn't matter who did it. In fact, several of the people Stalin would eventually get rid of could have attended these meetings as they had places on the various committees, but they simply couldn't be bothered to attend.

One of Stalin's jobs as General Secretary was to oversee the appointment and dismissal of Communist Party members to various positions in the regions of the USSR. Especially important were the job of secretary of a local branch and selecting who should be the local delegates to Party Congresses. This system of appointing rather than electing such people had started because of the disruptions of the Civil War; it helped Stalin because he could appoint his own supporters and demote or even expel those who were known to support his rivals. In this way, Stalin was eventually able to control the whole Party from the bottom up, and so become the next leader. 2/4

a

This answer scores half marks because:

► it gives **one well-explained reason** – Stalin's position as General Secretary of the Communist Party, which allowed him to control appointment to important Party positions;

► it uses **some detailed own knowledge** to support the argument: when he was given the job (1922); the types of appointments he could make; and how this had come about (the Civil War).

To score full marks, you also need to:

► give **at least two different explanations or reasons**. Other possible explanations:

i) The jealousy and resentment many Bolsheviks felt against Trotsky, who was seen as the most important leader after Lenin. Many resented the fact that he only joined the Bolshevik Party in 1917; also, he was quite arrogant towards those he believed were less gifted than himself.

ii) The fact that many of Stalin's supporters (not just Trotsky) seriously underestimated his ambition and cunning. In particular, Zinoviev and Kamenev thought that, as the important Communists in the Central Committee knew that Lenin had recommended that Stalin be dismissed, they could 'save' him and then use him to become the next leaders themselves.

iii) Trotsky's continued belief in Permanent (World) Revolution, with the prospect of continuing struggle and upheaval, seemed much less attractive than Stalin's idea of 'Socialism in One Country' which offered a period of calm and appealed to national pride.

► **use more specific own knowledge** (e.g. the answer could have referred to some of the leading Communists by name, such as Trotsky, Zinoviev, Kamenev and Bukharin).

(b) Study Source B. Why is the source useful as an explanation of the reasons for Stalin wanting to improve the Russian economy? [4 marks]

b

This source is useful in explaining why Stalin wanted to improve the Russian economy. First of all, it is from Stalin himself – by 1931, he was the ruler of Russia and so would know the state of the Russian economy. Also, the source itself says that Russia always has been backward, and still is – according to Stalin, it is at least 50 years behind more modern countries, and may be as much as 100 years behind. Stalin is worried about this because he is afraid that foreign countries might attack and defeat Russia as had happened in the past. So that is why he wanted to improve the Russian economy: 'Either we do it or they crush us.'

2/4

This answer scores half marks because:

► it makes **clear and precise reference to the source's content**, i.e. Russia's backwardness and Stalin's fear that it might be beaten again if the Russian economy is not quickly improved;

► it **uses the provenance information**: that it is from Stalin and that by 1931 he was in a position to know;

► it is **clearly focused on the usefulness** of the source – the word 'useful' is present.

To score full marks, you also need to:

► **give more than one explanation** – for instance, the source also suggests that it was a Communist duty to the working class to modernise the economy;

► **make use of precise own knowledge to support the reasons/explanations given** (e.g. you could refer to the **relative backwardness of Tsarist Russia** in 1914, or the **impact of the First World War and the Civil War**). Also important is the **USSR's isolation in the 1930s** and the fact that it had **been invaded twice since 1914**: by Germany in the First World War, and then by the Allies and Poland in the period 1918–1921.

DON'T MAKE THESE MISTAKES ...

✗ With 'why' or explanation questions, make sure you **don't just give vague or general own knowledge**. The Principal Examiner will be expecting you to **use plenty of relevant and specific own knowledge** to support the reasons you identify in your answer.

✗ When asked to explain some historical event or development, **never be satisfied with only talking about one reason**. If you do – even if you explain it and support it extremely well – you are limiting yourself to half marks at most. All significant historical developments will have several possible explanations, some of which will be linked. **So make sure you deal with at least two or three reasons**.

✗ When trying to explain the **usefulness** of a source, **never restrict yourself to only commenting on what the source says or shows (i.e. its content)**. If you do, you will limit yourself to the lower levels in the mark scheme. Instead, you must also discuss the **provenance/ attribution information provided**, and **bring in some own knowledge** to expand on or explain the significance of what the source contains.

Questions to try

Question 1 — EXAMINER'S HINTS

✔ This question asks you to consider **to what extent** a source explains a historical development, so make sure you show how it does AND how it does not – i.e. you need to write a balanced answer.

✔ Make sure you follow **all** the instructions in the question: in this case, you will have to **use the source AND your own knowledge**.

✔ Be careful – the question is about **industrial production**, so don't waste time writing about agriculture and collectivisation!

Study Source A. Use your own knowledge to explain whether the source explains fully how Stalin increased the industrial production of the USSR in the late 1920s and 1930s.

[8 marks]

SOURCE A
Graph of USSR's industrial output from 1927 to 1937 (in million tonnes).

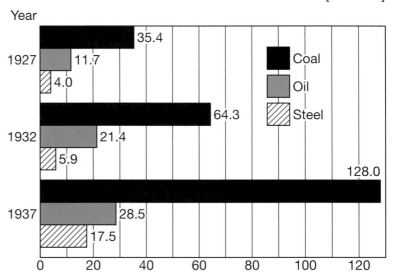

Question 2 — EXAMINER'S HINTS

✔ For this question, which asks you to **explain why Stalin introduced collectivisation** in the Soviet Union, you will need to examine a **range of different reasons**. Don't be satisfied with just writing about one.

✔ As this is an **explain** question, make sure you don't just produce a **list** of reasons. You must try to **show why/how these reasons were important**.

✔ If you can, **try to identify which reasons were more/less important**.

Why did Stalin introduce collectivisation? [6 marks]

Question 3

EXAMINER'S HINTS

✔ For **low-scoring questions** such as (a), **make a couple of quick points and then move on.** It is important not to write too much if the maximum marks available are only 2.

✔ When answering questions like (b), which ask you to assess the relative success/failure of some historical development, make sure you **attempt to produce a balanced answer.** Even if you want to say that something was successful, **you must still try to write about some things which were not so successful.**

✔ Also, try to **give specific/precise facts/details** when supporting your arguments: **general comments** such as 'The Five-Year Plans increased production a lot' **will not get you very far.**

These questions are about Stalin and the Soviet Union.

INFORMATION
This poster from 1928 says 'Industrialisation is the path to Socialism'.

(a) Describe briefly how Stalin tried to modernise Russia.
[2 marks]

(b) How successful were Stalin's economic policies by 1941? Explain your answer fully.
[5 marks]

ИНДУСТРИАЛИЗАЦИЯ
ПУТЬ к СОЦИАЛИЗМУ

Question 4   EXAMINER'S HINTS

✔ Remember – **pay attention to the number of marks available** for each question. For lower-scoring questions (2 or 3 marks), it is not necessary to write much more than about two or three sentences.

✔ With question (ii), **try to go beyond the details** of the trials themselves, **to consider their impact or function**.

✔ With questions (iii) and (iv), **make sure your answers cover a wide range of factors.** If you only write about one or two aspects, you will not get into the higher levels.

These questions are about Stalin's rule in the Soviet Union in the period 1928–1945. Look at the photograph below of a show trial and then answer the questions which follow.

(i)   Give ONE reason why Stalin developed the 'cult of personality'.   [3 marks]

(ii) Describe the key features of the show trials of the 1930s.   [5 marks]

(iii) Why did Stalin carry out a series of purges in the years to 1941?   [4 marks]

(iv) What were the effects of the purges on the Soviet Union in the years to 1941? [7 marks]

The answers can be found on pages **92–97.**

Key Dates to Remember

The USA, 1918–1941

1918	January	• President Woodrow Wilson (Democrat) issues his Fourteen Points
	November	• Republicans win control of the Senate
1919		• Congress refuses to join the League of Nations
1920	January	• Prohibition of alcohol
	May	• Sacco and Vanzetti Case begins a 'Red Scare'
	November	• Warren Harding (Republican) wins Presidential elections
1921		• Immigration Act
1922		• Fordney–McCumber Act puts high tariffs on foreign goods
1923		• Calvin Coolidge (Republican) becomes president – boom in speculation and share ownership
1924		• Immigration Act
		• Dawes Plan gives loans to Weimar Germany
1928	November	• Herbert Hoover (Republican) wins presidential elections – policies based on his belief in 'rugged individualism'
1929		• Immigration Act limits numbers even further
		• Young Plan gives further loans to Germany
	October	• Wall Street Crash and start of the Great Depression
1930		• Hawley–Smoot Tariffs introduced to increase import duties on foreign goods
1931		• Federal Farm Board buys wheat and cotton, but fails to stop fall in prices
1932		• Reconstruction Finance Corporation set up
	November	• Franklin Delano Roosevelt (Democrat) wins presidential elections, promising 'New Deal'
1933	March	• The First 100 Days – Roosevelt begins 'fireside chats'
	May	• First of the New Deal laws – the 'Alphabet Agencies'
		• Prohibition ended by the Twenty-first Amendment

45

1934		• First New Deal meets opposition • 'Dust Bowl' in the Mid-West
1935		• Roosevelt begins a Second New Deal
1936	**November**	• Roosevelt wins the presidential elections
1937		• USA experiences another Depression
1940	**November**	• Roosevelt wins a third term in the presidential elections
1941		• US agrees to Lend-Lease aid for Britain and the Soviet Union in their war against Nazi Germany
	December	• Japanese attack on Pearl Harbor brings the US into the Second World War

Mind Map

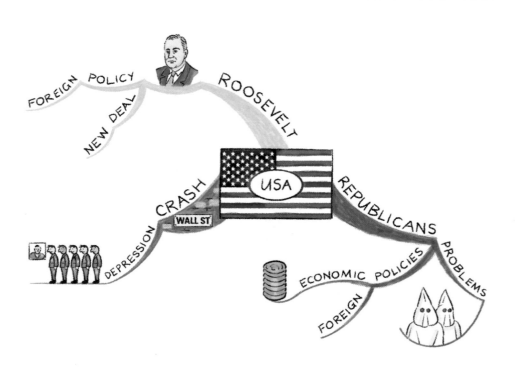

Exam Questions and Students' Answers

These questions are about the problems and challenges facing American society in the 1920s.

Study the sources below carefully and answer the questions which follow.

SOURCE A
A photograph of murdered gangsters, Chicago 1929.

SOURCE B
An American cartoon of 1924.

SOURCE C
Hiram Wesley Evans, Imperial Wizard of the Ku Klux Klan.

There are three great racial ideas which must be used to build up a great America: loyalty to the white race, to the traditions of America and to the spirit of Protestantism. The pioneer stock must be kept pure. The white race must be supreme not only in America but in the whole world. The Klan believes the Negroes are a special problem. Protestants must be supreme. The Roman Catholic Church is un-American and usually anti-American.

(a) What does Source A tell us about gangsters in the 1920s?

[2 marks]

The source tells us that these gangsters had been murdered, so there must have been a lot of violence in Chicago at that time: in the photograph, there appear to be at least five bodies. However, the photograph is only of one city in one year, so we can't assume that it was as violent in every city in the USA or that the 1920s as a whole were like this.

½

(b) What information does Source B give about immigration into the USA?

[3 marks]

Source B shows us that a lot of people from Europe were trying to get into the USA in 1924, and that the USA (represented by the figure of 'Uncle Sam') was trying to stop this by only letting in 3% of those who wanted to come.

⅓

(c) According to Source C, what were the aims of the Ku Klux Klan?

[4 marks]

Source C shows us that the Ku Klux Klan's aims were to make the whites supreme, not just in the USA but also in the whole world. To do this, they believed that it would be necessary to protect the Protestant religion from the Catholic Church, and to keep the white race pure in order to keep up the traditions of America. They would do this by attacking blacks (negroes).

²/4

Questions (a), (b) and (c)

These three questions require you to show that you understand and can explain the information provided by a source.

> **The three answers score half marks – or less – because:**

▶ **they give reasonably full descriptions, or paraphrases**, of what the sources say or show.

> **To score full marks with such questions, you need to:**

▶ go beyond the obvious information provided by the sources, and **add some of your own knowledge about the topics to explain fully what is in the sources.**

> **For (a), you need to:**

▶ **link the evidence of violence provided by the photograph to the history of gangsterism in the USA during the 1920s and 1930s.** For example, mention of the growth of powerful gangs as a result of Prohibition, and the emergence of gang leaders such as Al Capone and Bugs Moran, would be enough to get full marks. It would not be necessary to say that the photograph was, in fact, of the St Valentine's Day Massacre – though if you did, this too would get that extra mark.

▶ As this is **not a question about the usefulness** of the source, **the comments on the typicality of the source, though valid, do not help explain the background** of the source and so do not lead to the highest level.

> **In (b), you need to:**

▶ **use your own knowledge to show how this cartoon refers to attempts by US governments in the 1920s to control the number of immigrants into the USA by a system of quotas.** As well as the 1924 Act mentioned in the cartoon, there had been the Emergency Quota Act in 1921; and another Immigration Act was later passed in 1929. These were, in part, a result of the 'Red Scare' which developed in the United States, as foreigners were seen by some as bringing in 'alien' political ideas from Europe, such as socialism and anarchism.

> **In (c), you need to:**

▶ **try to make some general comment on, or summary of, the content of the source**, e.g. this extract is all about the Ku Klux Klan's attempt to secure white domination in the USA.

▶ **use your own knowledge** to explain that the KKK was racist, and how it grew in the 1920s – by 1925, it had about 5 million members (mostly in the southern states). It campaigned, often using great violence against blacks and others (especially recent Catholic immigrants from southern Europe), for the 'preservation' of the WASP (White, Anglo-Saxon, Protestant) lifestyle.

DON'T MAKE THESE MISTAKES ...

✘ Just describing or paraphrasing what a particular source shows or says will only get you **half marks** at most. You need to assume that the examiner marking your answer is also able to understand what information a particular source is giving!

✘ So, when answering source comprehension questions like these, try to go beyond listing what the source is showing and, instead, **make a general comment on the content AND use a little of your own knowledge** to place the source in its historical context/background.

Questions to try

Question 1   EXAMINER'S HINTS

✔ For Question 1(i), try to show how Source C **both supports and does not support the other two sources** – and make sure you **make references to all three sources**.

✔ For Question 1(ii), make sure you use the **three sources AND your own knowledge**. If you only do one of these tasks, you will only get half marks at most.

This question is about President Hoover and the Depression.
Study Sources A, B and C carefully and then answer the questions below.

SOURCE A
From a school textbook about the Depression in the USA written in 1986.

Soon after Hoover became President, the USA was hit by economic depression. President Hoover was unwilling to spend government money to boost the economy. He argued that the role of the government was that of referee rather than player. He believed the USA had been prosperous in the 1920s because of the government policy of non-interference. He thought that it was simply a matter of time before trade revived.

Economic depression cannot be cured by government laws or presidential statements. The economic wounds must be healed by the producers and consumers themselves.

SOURCE B
From a speech by President Hoover in 1930.

SOURCE C
From a school textbook about the history of the USA published in 1984.

In January 1932, the US government introduced the Reconstruction Finance Corporation (RFC). This was a government agency designed to make loans to banks, insurance companies and construction companies. Hoover saw the RFC as an emergency measure to be used with care and for no longer than two years. He felt that it would bring back confidence to the USA.

(i) Does Source C support the evidence of Sources A and B? Explain your answer.

[4 marks]

(ii) Why was there opposition to Hoover's policies in the years 1929–33?
Use Sources A, B and C, and your own knowledge, to explain your answer.   [6 marks]

Question 2

EXAMINER'S HINTS

✔ Try to **make detailed use of the source** – and make sure you deal with the source specified in the question!

✔ Try to **give a balanced response** – so look for evidence in the source which might support a 'yes' and a 'no' view.

SOURCE D
The views of two historians on the Immigration Laws of the 1920s.

> *Statement 1*
> *Immigration Laws were introduced on a quota system to reduce the number of foreign immigrants coming into the USA. The new mood of isolation after the war brought concerns about the previous 'open door' policy. It was now felt that this had allowed too many foreigners to come into America without any controls.*
>
> *Statement 2*
> *Immigration was reduced by the quota system. There were fears that the new immigrants took jobs away from 'real Americans'. There was a further fear that new immigrants would bring with them different political ideas which could threaten American democracy.*

Use Source D only. Do the two statements agree on the reasons for the introduction of the Immigration Laws in the USA in the 1920s? Give reasons for your answers.

[4 marks]

The answers can be found on pages **98–100.**

Key Dates to Remember

International relations, 1918–1939

1918	January	• Wilson's Fourteen Points – Point 14 calls for the establishment of an international organisation
1919	June	• Conference of Ambassadors
1919–20		• Peace treaties' first 26 articles set up the League of Nations' Covenant
1920	January	• League of Nations set up, with headquarters at Geneva
	September	• War between Turkey and Greece begins
1920–21		• Dispute between Poland and Lithuania over Vilna
		• Russo–Polish War
1921	March	• Dispute over Upper Silesia between Germany and Poland
1922	February	• Washington Naval Treaty
	March	• Genoa Conference on Disarmament
	December	• War between Turkey and Greece ends
1923	January	• Invasion of Ruhr by France and Belgium
		• Alliance between France and Czechoslovakia
	August	• Corfu crisis between Italy and Greece
		• Dawes Plan
1924	September	• Geneva Protocol drawn up
1924–25		• Dispute over the Mosul area between Iraq and Turkey
1925	October	• Geneva Protocol rejected
		• Locarno Treaty
		• War between Greece and Bulgaria
1926	September	• Germany allowed to join League of Nations
1928	August	• Kellogg-Briand Pact (Pact of Paris)
1929	October	• Death of Stresemann
		• Wall Street Crash

1931	September	● Japanese invasion of Manchuria
	December	● Lytton Commission sent to investigate by the League – Conference of Ambassadors is dissolved
1932	February	● League of Nations' Disarmament Conference
1933	January	● Hitler becomes Chancellor of Germany
	February	● Japan leaves the League of Nations
	October	● Germany leaves Disarmament Conference and League of Nations
	November	● Germany begins re-armament
1934	January	● Disarmament Conference ends in failure
		● German–Polish Non-Aggression Pact
	July	● Hitler attempts *Anschluss* with Austria
	September	● Soviet Union joins League of Nations
1935	March	● Saarland votes to return to Germany, and Hitler reintroduces conscription
	April	● Stresa Front between Britain, France and Italy
	June	● Anglo–German Naval Agreement
	October	● Italy invades Abyssinia
	December	● Hoare–Laval Pact
1936	March	● Hitler orders re-occupation of the Rhineland
	August	● Hitler and Mussolini support Franco as Spanish Civil War begins
		● Hitler's 4-Year War Plan
	October	● Rome–Berlin Axis
	November	● Anti-Comintern Pact (Germany and Japan)
1937	May	● Neville Chamberlain becomes British Prime Minister (promising appeasement)
	July	● Japan attacks China
	October	● Italy signs Anti-Comintern Pact (Rome–Berlin–Tokyo Axis)
	December	● Italy leaves the League of Nations
1938	March	● *Anschluss* between Germany and Austria
	September	● Sudeten Crisis and Munich Conference
1939	March	● Hitler invades rest of Czechoslovakia
	May	● Pact of Steel (Germany and Italy)
	August	● Nazi–Soviet Non-Aggression (Molotov–Ribbentrop) Pact
	September	● German invasion of Poland

Exam Questions and Students' Answers

1 (a) What were the functions of the Assembly and of the Council of the League of Nations? **[4 marks]**

1a

These bodies of the League of Nations, which had been insisted on by President Woodrow Wilson of the USA in his Fourteen Points, were supposed to keep the peace at the end of the First World War. They did this by trying to sort out international disputes, and could put economic sanctions on countries who resorted to war. 2/4

(b) Explain why some major nations were not members of the League when it was first set up. **[6 marks]**

1b

There were several major nations which did not join the League of Nations when it was first set up. The three most important countries which did not join were the USA, Germany and Russia. The reasons they did not join were all different. The USA did not join, even though its president (Woodrow Wilson) wanted it to join, because joining was not popular in the US. Germany was not allowed to join and nor was Russia. 3/6

(c) 'The most important reason why the League was weak was that it made decisions very slowly.' Do you agree with this statement? Explain your answer. **[10 marks]**

1c

I agree with this statement about the League of Nations making decisions very slowly. This was why it was so weak, because international disputes got worse while the League was trying to agree on what to do. This was shown in two crises – the Japanese invasion of Manchuria in 1931, and Italy's invasion of Abyssinia in 1935. In both cases, the League failed to prevent or stop aggression, or to solve the problems. If the League had acted more quickly (for instance, it took a year for its Lytton Commission to make a report and suggestions on what to do about Japan's attack on Manchuria), then it might have succeeded. One reason it was slow to act was because it didn't meet very frequently; another reason was that important decisions had to be unanimous. This slowness only encouraged strong countries to think they too could get away with aggression – especially Germany when Hitler took over. 5/10

Question **1a** asks you to describe the functions of the two most important bodies of the League of Nations.

This answer scores half marks because:

► it identifies two general functions of the League.

To score full marks, you also need to:

► **clearly separate the two bodies mentioned, and indicate their different functions.** The Assembly could recommend action to the Council, vote to accept new members and approve or reject the League's budget; the Council could attempt to solve international disputes, decide if a particular country was being aggressive and, if its recommendations were ignored, could impose economic sanctions against the aggressor.

► **include more specific/detailed information** – e.g. the Assembly met once a year in Geneva, with every member having one vote and votes for action having to be unanimous; while the Council was made up of the 'Big Four' (Britain, France, Italy and Japan), along with a few other countries which changed from time to time.

Question **1b** requires you to explain why some important countries did not join the League.

This answer scores half marks because:

► **it clearly identifies three countries which did not join, and gives brief/ general – but correct – explanations of why each one did not join.**

To score full marks, you also need to:

► **give fuller/more detailed explanations of why each one did not join** – e.g. the US did not join because the US Congress rejected the Treaty of Versailles and believed membership of the League would prove costly if the US had to help sort out problems all over the world. This was an indication of growing isolationism in the US, which affected many Americans, especially the Republicans. Germany was not allowed to join until it had proved itself as a peaceful country (it was allowed to join in 1926); while Russia was not allowed to join because it was ruled by the Bolsheviks and all other European countries feared the spread of Communism.

Question **1c** asks you to decide why the League was weak AND to make a judgement about the relevant importance of the different reasons.

This answer scores half marks because:

► **it gives a reasonably full explanation of one factor** (the slowness of the League to make decisions, as mentioned in the question's statement) contributing to the League's weakness;

► it attempts to address the question by **giving clear support for the statement.**

To score full marks, you also need to:

► **consider a variety/range of different factors, in addition to the one given in the question, to explain the weakness of the League** – e.g. how many countries didn't trust it as it was seen as a club for the 'victors' of the First World War, intended to police the Treaty of Versailles; its lack of any armed forces of its own; how the non-membership of important nations, such as the US, Germany and the Soviet Union, made it difficult to impose economic sanctions; the tendency of Britain and France to weaken and undermine the League by giving more importance to their own interests; and how the economic depression of the 1930s led to the rise of extreme nationalist governments determined to follow expansionist and aggressive foreign policies in an attempt to solve their economic problems;

► **try to show the inter-relationship between these different factors, and how no one factor** – even though it might possibly be more important than the others – **can give a full/complete explanation** of the weakness of the League.

2 Study the source carefully, and then answer the question which follows.

SOURCE A
A photograph of a crowd in Austria on the arrival of the German army, March 1938.

Look at Source A. What does the source tell you about Austrian reactions to the German occupation of their country? Explain your answer, referring to details of the source.

[4 marks]

The photograph shows clearly that the Austrian people approved of the German occupation of their country – what Hitler and the Nazis called the Anschluss (union) of two German-speaking countries. But this only shows some Austrians, and some people might have felt differently.

2/4

This question asks you to show you have understood the information given by a source, and to pick out specific details to support your comments.

This answer scores half marks because:

► it does give a general interpretation of what the source seems to be showing.

To score full marks, you also need to:

► **make a detailed use of the source** – i.e. refer to some of the following: the smiling faces, the number of people giving the Nazi salute, the swastika flags and the fact that a soldier is having to hold the crowd back, as all being proof that they approved.

DON'T MAKE THESE MISTAKES ...

✗ With straightforward 'describe' questions, **don't just make one or two general comments** – the examiner will be looking for specific/detailed items of information.

✗ When you are asked **to comment on the relative importance of several factors, make sure you do so,** even if it is only a tentative comment – **if you don't, you'll not reach the top level.**

✗ When answering 'why' questions, make sure you:
- **don't just describe** what the question has asked you to explain;
- **give plenty of different reasons and detailed explanations** – i.e. give specific facts to show why something happened;
- **don't just give a list of reasons** – each reason will need to be explained or supported with plenty of facts.

Mind Map

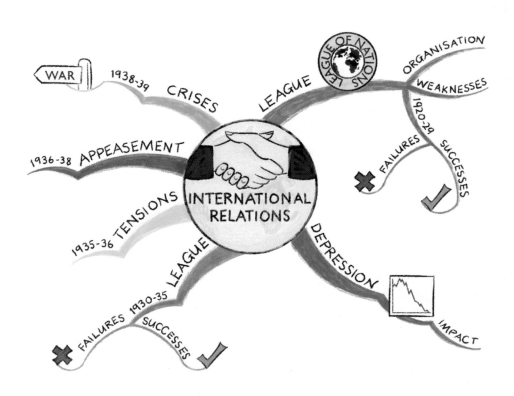

Questions to try

Question 1

EXAMINER'S HINTS

✔ This question asks you to decide which of two sources provides a more reliable view of the League of Nations' actions during the Abyssinian Crisis, **so make sure you comment about both of the sources** AND that you **indicate which one you think is more reliable.**

✔ Also, the question asks you to use your own knowledge: remember – **if you only talk about the sources OR your own knowledge, you will only score half marks or even less.**

Study Sources A and B below, and then answer the question which follows.

SOURCE A
A cartoon from the British magazine, *Punch*, in 1935. *Punch* was usually very patriotic and rarely criticised British foreign policy.

THE AWFUL WARNING.

FRANCE AND ENGLAND (*together?*). "WE DON'T WANT YOU TO FIGHT, BUT, BY JINGO, IF YOU DO, WE SHALL PROBABLY ISSUE A JOINT MEMORANDUM SUGGESTING A MILD DISAPPROVAL OF YOU."

SOURCE B
Comments on the Abyssinian Crisis, said by Anthony Eden, British Foreign Minister, to a meeting of the British Cabinet in May 1936.

Could the League survive the failure of sanctions to rescue Abyssinia? Could it ever impose sanctions again? Probably there had never been such a clear-cut case for sanctions. If the League failed in this case there could probably be no confidence that it could succeed again in the future.

Which source gives a more reliable view of the reactions of the League of Nations to the Italian invasion of Abyssinia in October 1935? Refer to Sources A and B, and your own knowledge, to explain your answer.

[10 marks]

Question 2   EXAMINER'S HINTS

✔ This question is asking you to comment on whether the two sources provide sufficient information on why Japan was able to complete its invasion of Manchuria. **As two sources are mentioned, you must make sure you say something about both of them.**

✔ You also need to **use your own knowledge** to help you decide whether these two sources do provide sufficient information. As well as making sure you do add facts, **remember to give specific details rather than making general comments.**

Study Sources C and D below, and answer the question which follows.

SOURCE C
A view about the Manchurian Crisis of 1931, taken from a history textbook published in 1954.

The Japanese Government could count on the ignorance of people too busy with difficulties at home to be bothered about events in remote lands. People's minds in both America and Europe were with the economic depression that had started in 1929 and was at its worst in 1931–32.

SOURCE D
A cartoon by David Low, showing Japan as a gangster who is able to defy the League of Nations over the invasion of Manchuria in 1931.

Do Sources C and D provide enough information to explain why Japan was able to complete its invasion of Manchuria in 1931? Use both the sources and your own knowledge to explain your answer.

[6 marks]

Key Dates to Remember

The Second World War

1939	September	● Germany invades Poland
	October	● Start of the 'Phoney War'
1940	April	● End of 'Phoney War'; Germany occupies Denmark and invades Norway
	May	● Norway surrenders; the Netherlands, Belgium and Luxembourg are defeated; Germany invades France; British evacuation at Dunkirk
	June	● Italy declares war on Britain and France; France surrenders to Germany; Britain stands alone (until June 1941)
	August	● Start of the Battle of Britain
	September–October	● Italy invades Egypt and Greece
	December	● Britain defeats Italy in Egypt and takes Libya
1941	March	● US Lend-Lease Scheme to Britain begins; Battle of the Atlantic begins
	April	● Germany invades Yugoslavia and Greece (to help Italy); Rommel recaptures Libya and invades Egypt
	May	● Greece and Yugoslavia are defeated
	June	● Germany invades the Soviet Union ('Operation Barbarossa')
	July	● Japan invades French Indochina; the USA places a trade embargo on Japan
	December	● The Russian Red Army counter-attacks on the Eastern Front; after the Japanese attack on Pearl Harbor, USA enters the war
1942	May	● Rommel defeats Britain at the battle of Tobruk
	June	● US naval victory at the battle of Midway
	October–November	● Montgomery defeats Rommel at the battle of el Alamein
	November	● Start of the battle of Stalingrad

1943	January	● Red Army wins the battle of Stalingrad
	May	● Victory for Allied 'Operation Torch' in North Africa
	July	● Red Army wins battle of Kursk; Allies invade Sicily
	September	● Allied invasion of mainland Italy; Mussolini overthrown; Red Army forces German retreat on the Eastern Front
1944	January	● US start 'island hopping' strategy in the Pacific
	March	● Germany defeated in the Battle of the Atlantic
	June	● D-Day ('Operation Overlord'); USSR launches a new offensive in the east
	December	● Battle of the Bulge
1945	March	● US begin massive bombing of mainland Japan
	May	● Red Army enters Berlin; Hitler commits suicide, and Germany surrenders
	July	● Japan rejects armistice; USSR joins war against Japan
	August	● US drop atomic bombs on Hiroshima and Nagasaki; Japan surrenders; end of the war

Mind Map

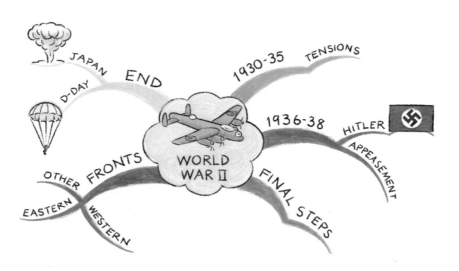

Exam Question and Student's Answer

The question below is about the war on the Eastern Front in the period 1941–1945.
Study the table below and then answer the question which follows.

1941	'Operation Barbarossa'
1942	Red Army's counter-offensive
1942–43	Battle of Stalingrad
1943	Battle of Kursk

Why was the German army unable to defeat the Soviet Union in the period 1941–1945?

[8 marks]

1

The German army was unable to defeat the Soviet Union in the period 1941-45 because of the Russian winter. Hitler had planned his attack on the Soviet Union – code-named 'Operation Barbarossa' – to start earlier than the actual start, which was in June 1941. He had always intended to invade the Soviet Union and, in December 1940, had decided the attack should begin in the spring of 1941, so that the fighting would be over before the Russian winter began.

This delay was because Hitler's allies, the Italians, had performed badly in Greece and the Balkans, and Hitler had been forced to divert troops to help them. In addition, bad weather also delayed the start, and Hitler failed to build extra airfields closer to the USSR. But, despite these delays, Hitler was convinced his forces could defeat the Red Army, and the first stages of the invasion seemed to prove him right. Stalin had ignored intelligence warnings that Nazi Germany was about to attack, as he believed Hitler would not attack until Britain had been defeated first. As a result, many

Russian military units were not prepared – most of the Soviet air force was destroyed on the ground, and over 700,000 Red Army troops were captured. The Soviet forces suffered tremendous defeats and, by October 1941, the collapse of the USSR seemed inevitable.

However, the Russian winter came earlier than expected, and was very severe. The German advance was slowed, first by rain and mud, and then by snow and extremely low temperatures. But, because Hitler had expected to defeat the USSR before the winter began, German troops were not equipped for a winter campaign. As a result, German soldiers suffered from frostbite, while machinery and fuel froze. This then allowed the Red Army to launch their first counter-attack in December 1941. This eventually resulted in important victories for the Red Army at Stalingrad and Kursk in 1943. After that, the Red Army began to force the Germans into a retreat.

3/8

This answer scores 3 marks because:

▶ **it does attempt to answer the question** – i.e. the student does not simply write down all she knows about the topic, in the hope that some of it will be relevant. This is not simply a descriptive/narrative-type answer, which is something many students produce under exam pressure.

▶ **it correctly identifies one reason** why the German army was unable to defeat the Soviet Union in the period mentioned in the question – the impact of the Russian winter on the ability of German troops to maintain their early successes in 'Operation Barbarossa'. However, this candidate has not fully answered the question, as only one reason is given, while other factors/ turning points – including those listed in the table – are not dealt with.

To score full marks, you also need to:

▶ **mention and briefly explain a range of factors** – e.g. as the Germans invaded rapidly, the Russians retreated and successfully moved over 4000 factories and 10 million workers to safety behind the Ural Mountains, which meant war production could continue. This was also helped by Stalin's Five-Year Plans, which had rapidly built up Soviet industry. As a result, the USSR was able to continue and even increase weapons production during the war. Also, Stalin ordered a 'scorched earth' policy, which denied the German Army valuable resources. In addition, because the German supply lines soon became badly stretched, the Russians were able to use partisan (resistance) units to attack behind enemy lines. Other reasons for the German failure include the brutal Nazi treatment of Soviet civilians, which enabled Stalin to unite most Russians behind him in what became known as the 'Great Patriotic War'. Also useful were the experienced Siberian troops, who were experts in winter warfare. The Lend-Lease agreement with the USA was also important in getting supplies to the USSR – especially after the USA entered the war in December 1941. Another important factor was that Stalin usually left military decisions to his commanders, such as General Zhukov, while Hitler (who became increasingly fanatical about defeating the USSR) frequently interfered. This included splitting his forces in 1942, which helped the Red Army to surround and defeat the German Sixth Army at Stalingrad in January 1943.

► **say something about all the factors mentioned in the table** – e.g. the Soviet victory in July 1943 at the Battle of Kursk was a crucial turning point, as this great tank battle (the biggest in history) was the last major German offensive on the Eastern Front; this enabled the Red Army to go on the offensive, pushing the Germans out of Russia and eastern Europe and, eventually, back into Germany.

DON'T MAKE THESE MISTAKES ...

✗ **Don't lose sight of what the question is about** and instead write about something that is only vaguely connected. Even if your facts are plentiful and correct, you will at best only score 1 or 2 marks, and you may not score any marks at all.

✗ Remember – with 'why' questions you must focus on **giving a range of reasons/explanations**. You must also make sure you **give plenty of precise examples** to support your points – general assertions will only get half marks at most.

Questions to try

Question 1

EXAMINER'S HINTS

✔ **Make sure you give specific examples of cross-references;** do not simply give a general one involving all three sources.

✔ **Do not cross-reference the wrong sources** – this is a mistake often made by candidates in History exams.

✔ **Try to look for disagreements as well as agreements.**

SOURCE A
A description by Erwin Rommel, one of Germany's leading commanders in the Second World War, about the advance of the German armies into Poland, September 1939.

> *The tanks now rolled in a long column through the line of fortification and on towards the first houses, which had been set alight by our fire. Occasionally an enemy machine-gun or anti-tank gun fired, but none of these came anywhere near us. Gradually the speed increased. Before long we were 1000, 2000, 3000 metres into the fortified zone. On we went, at a steady speed, towards our objective.*

SOURCE C
From a modern history textbook about the Second World War published in 1984. This extract describes the fall of Poland in September 1939.

SOURCE B
A diagram showing the German tactic of Blitzkrieg.

> *The German armies moved forward quickly. They were helped by the German air force. Stuka dive-bombers found that the Polish troops were easy targets. The Poles had little chance. They were outnumbered. Their weapons were out of date. Their armies retreated in confusion. But they fought with bravery. On 6 September, Polish horsemen made a cavalry charge on German tanks, and Polish pilots crashed their planes into German bombers.*

Does Source C support the evidence of Sources A and B about the reasons for the defeat of Poland? Explain your answer.

[6 marks]

Question 2

EXAMINER'S HINTS

✔ Remember – **pay attention to the number of marks available** for each question. The higher the mark, the more you will need to write.

✔ Make sure you **use your own knowledge**, as well as the relevant sources, to explain your answers

✔ With question (i), try to go beyond the face-value details of the sources; instead, try to **make deductions and/or point out limitations of the sources**.

✔ With question (ii), make sure your answer contains a **range of different explanations**, including comments on the **possible bias/motives/purposes** of the authors.

Study these sources, which are about the war in the Pacific in the period 1944–1945. Then answer the questions which follow.

SOURCE A
American and Japanese casualty figures in battles for the Pacific Islands.

Year	Battle location	United States	Japan
1944	Leyte	17,000	78,000
1945	Luzon	35,000	156,000
1945	Iwo Jima	20,000	22,000

SOURCE B
Adapted from a speech by James Byrne, the US Secretary of State, made in 1945.

Any weapon that would bring an end to the war and save a million casualties among the Americans was justified. The Japanese hadn't hesitated at Pearl Harbor to make a sneak attack, destroying not only our ships but the lives of many American sailors. I believed that the atom bomb would be successful and would force the Japanese to accept surrender on our terms.

SOURCE C
Adapted from *The Roots of European Security*, by the Soviet historian V. Nekasov, published in 1984.

The Americans claimed that the bombing of Hiroshima was aimed at bringing the end of the war nearer and avoiding unnecessary bloodshed and casualties. But they had entirely different objectives. The purpose of the bombings was to frighten other countries, above all the Soviet Union. It has since involved the world in a nuclear arms race.

(i) Study Sources A and B and use your own knowledge. Do the figures in Source A support the view given in the first sentence of Source B? Give reasons for your answer.

[5 marks]

(ii) Study Sources B and C and use your own knowledge. These two sources differ in their interpretation of why the USA dropped the atom bomb in 1945. Why do you think they differ in this way? Explain your answer. [10 marks]

The answers can be found on pages **103–105**.

Key Dates to Remember

Britain, 1900–1945

1903	● Formation of the WSPU, led by the Pankhursts
1906	● Liberals win election and begin reforms ● WSPU begins militant campaign
1908	● Old Age Pensions Act
1909	● 'People's Budget' rejected by Lords ● Force-feeding of hunger-striking suffragettes begins
1911	● Parliament Act
1912	● Home Rule Bill passed by Commons ● WSPU begins a more violent campaign
1913	● Cat and Mouse Act ● Formation of 'Triple Industrial Alliance'
1914	● Home Rule Act becomes law, but the start of First World War leads to its suspension ● WSPU ends protests ● DORA gives emergency powers to government
1915	● Recruitment campaign starts; women fill labour shortages ● First Zeppelin raids
1916	● Start of compulsory conscription ● Easter Rebellion in Dublin
1917	● Germans use bombers instead of Zeppelins ● Voluntary rationing introduced ● Formation of women's sections of the armed forces
1918	● Rationing made compulsory ● Women over 30 are given the vote ● Sinn Fein, led by de Valera, wins Irish elections; start of Irish 'War of Independence'
1920	● Start of post-war slump
1921	● Unemployment Insurance Act starts 'dole' payments ● Stalemate in Ireland leads to ceasefire
1922	● Partition Treaty ends war in Ireland; Ireland divided into two
1925	● 'Red Friday' – government gives subsidy to mine owners to prevent wage-cuts
1926	● General Strike ends after nine days

1929	• MacDonald leads second Labour government
	• Economic crisis follows US Wall Street Crash
1931	• May Committee suggests cuts; formation of National Government
1934	• Unemployment Insurance Act brings in the 'means test'
1935	• MacDonald resigns, and is replaced by Baldwin, leader of the Conservatives
1936	• Jarrow Crusade
1937	• ARP wardens recruited
1938	• Conscription of men aged 20–21; gas masks issued
1939	• Start of Second World War; conscription for all men aged 19–41
1940	• The Battle of Britain. Local Defence Volunteers become the Home Guard
	• Start of the Blitz; evacuation is increased. Start of rationing
1941	• All single women 19–30 conscripted for the war effort
1944	• V1 attacks
1945	• V2 attacks; end of the war

Mind Map

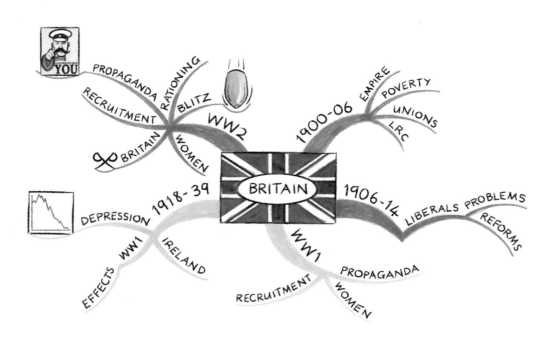

Exam Questions and Students' Answers

This question is about life in the Depression.
Study the information below and answer the questions which follow.

INFORMATION
For many families,
life in the depressed
areas during the
1930s was very
difficult.

1 (a) What popular name was given to the money given to the unemployed by the
government during the 1930s?   [1 mark]

*The benefit paid to the long-term unemployed was called the
'dole'.*   ¹⁄₁

(b) Name **one** area in Wales which suffered from high unemployment during the
1930s.   [1 mark]

*The Rhondda, in south Wales, was one of the worst-hit areas in
Wales during the 1930s.*   ¹⁄₁

These answers score full marks because:

► **there is correct factual recall** concerning (a) the 'dole' and
(b) the correct identification of one area in Wales.

(c) Describe what was meant by the term *means test*.   [2 marks]

*The means test was a test for unemployment benefits which
was brought in by the National Government in 1934 by the
Unemployment Insurance Act, as part of the 'economy drive'
recommended by the May Committee in 1931, to cope with the*

effects of the Depression. This was at a time when almost 3 million people were unemployed. With the means test, the amount of benefit paid to an unemployed man would depend on the total income of his family, including pensions and savings. This was checked by the new Unemployment Assistance Board set up by the Act. If a son or daughter had a regular job, the father would get no 'dole' payment at all, as it was assumed his children would support him. Even if a school child had a paper round, the money had to be declared and was knocked off the amount of 'dole' which would be paid. This system saved the government several million pounds a year, but caused great hardship and resentment in the depressed areas.

²⁄₂

(d) Why were there hunger marches during this period?   [3 marks]

1d

There were hunger marches during the Depression because the unemployed wanted to protest about the hardship and humiliation caused by the means test. They usually took place in the most depressed areas, such as the North-east of England, Lancashire, west Cumberland (Cumbria), south Wales and Scotland. One of the most famous ones was the Jarrow Crusade in 1936. This was when 200 men marched from Jarrow to London to present a petition to the government. Many of these hunger marches were organised by the National Unemployed Workers' Movement (NUWM); this had been set up in 1921 and, at first, had involved the Labour Party but, during the Depression, the Communist Party became the main organisers. There were often clashes between the marchers and the police.

²⁄₃

(e) Why did so many people leave Wales during this period?   [4 marks]

1e

The reason so many people left Wales during the Depression was because there was so much unemployment there in the 1930s as a result of the Wall Street Crash. This was because in areas such as south Wales, most people worked in the older 'staple' industries such as coal, iron, steel, shipbuilding and textiles. When the Depression hit, these were the industries which suffered most, so unemployment in such regions was highest and long-term. Because there was very little other industry, many people thought it best to move to areas where there were different industries and where unemployment was therefore lower.

2/4

This answer scores full marks because:

► **it gives a *correct* explanation of what the means test was** (i.e. it was a special income test which determined how much unemployment benefit would be paid to the long-term unemployed);

► **there is plenty of *detailed* supporting factual information** which explains how the means test worked.

This answer scores two marks because:

► **it clearly identifies *one* reason** why there were hunger marches (protest against the means test);

► it gives **detailed facts which *explain* and *support*** this reason.

To score full marks, you also need to:

► **give more than one explanation**, e.g. the hunger marches were also designed as political events: to draw attention to the impact of unemployment; to pressurise the government into taking action; and to push for new investment and industries for their areas.

This answer scores two marks because: 1e

► **it gives one explanation of why so many left Wales**, i.e. that it was because of the high unemployment in many areas, such as south Wales;

► **there is some accurate and detailed supporting information**.

To score full marks, you also need to:

► **give a fuller and more balanced explanation**, which means trying to think of **more than one reason**; for instance, significant unemployment in south Wales before the start of the Depression; many of the 'staple' industries had been in decline; the general attraction of the new industries in England, such as chemicals, electronics, and the car and aircraft industries.

DON'T MAKE THESE MISTAKES ...

✗ **With low-scoring questions, don't give lots of supporting facts.** This will not gain you extra marks and will mean you are wasting time.

✗ **Read questions carefully** – if it asks you **'why'** something happened or was important, you will not score highly if all you do is describe the event or importance.

✗ Also **with 'why' questions, never just give one explanation** – the Principal Examiner will be expecting you to be able to give **at least two or three**. If you can only remember lots of facts about one reason, then at least refer briefly to one or two more.

Questions to try

This question is about the campaign for women's suffrage.

Look carefully at Sources A to E and then answer the questions below.

SOURCE A
From a suffragist postcard from the early twentieth century.

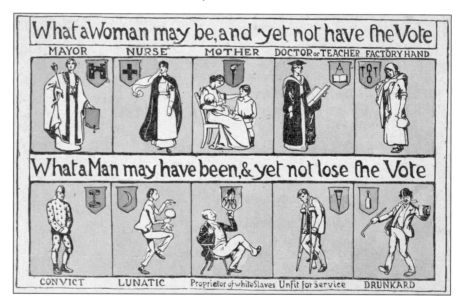

SOURCE B
From *Votes For Women*, a study by D. Atkinson, 1988. It describes the first violence used by the WSPU in 1908.

On 30 June 1908 thousands of sympathisers and members of the public went to a demonstration organised by the WSPU in Parliament Square, London. Five thousand police were called in to deal with the crowds, and violence broke out. Enraged by the violence in the Square, two teachers, both WSPU members, took a cab into Downing Street and flung small stones through the windows of the Prime Minister's house. Twenty-seven women were sent to prison that day, and the first window-smashers served two months in Holloway Prison. When they were released they were treated like heroines by the suffragettes.

SOURCE C
From *The Daily Express*, 14 October 1908.

The time for gently dealing with idle, mischievous women who call themselves 'militant suffragists' has gone. The important business of the State has been held up. Hundreds of policemen were given difficult and unnecessary work. Such things cannot be tolerated. Now the country will demand that these women, who encourage disorder and riot, should be punished with the utmost severity.

SOURCE D
A map of suffragette activities in June 1913.

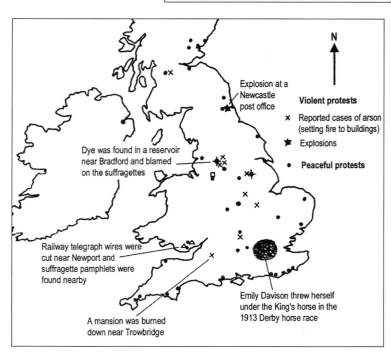

N

Explosion at a Newcastle post office

Violent protests

× Reported cases of arson (setting fire to buildings)

★ Explosions

● **Peaceful protests**

Dye was found in a reservoir near Bradford and blamed on the suffragettes

Railway telegraph wires were cut near Newport and suffragette pamphlets were found nearby

A mansion was burned down near Trowbridge

Emily Davison threw herself under the King's horse in the 1913 Derby horse race

SOURCE E
From *Unshackled*, by Christabel Pankhurst, 1950.

If Mrs Fawcett and my mother, Emmeline Pankhurst, had worked together in the years before the First World War, the House of Commons might have agreed to their demands. The Prime Minister could not easily have fought both wings of the Women's Movement.

(a) What can you learn from Source A about why suffragists thought that women should have the vote?

[4 marks]

(b) Do Sources B and D support the view about suffragette activity given in Source C? Explain your answer using all three sources.

[4 marks]

(c) Explain why women failed to achieve the vote in parliamentary elections in the period before 1914. Use Sources C, D and E, and your own knowledge, to explain your answer.

[6 marks]

The answers can be found on pages **106–108**.

Key Dates to Remember

The Cold War, 1945–1991

1945	March	● Yalta Conference
	July	● Potsdam Conference
	August	● US drops atomic bombs on Hiroshima and Nagasaki

1946	March	● Churchill's 'Iron Curtain' speech
1947	January	● Britain and US merge their German zones to form 'Bizonia'
	March	● Truman Doctrine announced
	June	● Marshall Plan announced
1948	June	● Start of Berlin Crisis – Soviet Blockade and US–GB Airlift
1949	April	● NATO set up
	August	● Soviet A-bomb tested
	October	● Chinese Communists take power
1950	June	● Start of Korean War
1952	November	● US explodes H-bomb
1953	July	● USSR explodes an H-bomb
		● North and South Korea sign an armistice
1954	May	● French defeated at Dien Bien Phu
	July	● Geneva Accords – Vietnam temporarily divided along 17th Parallel

1955	February	● Khrushchev emerges as main Soviet leader – calls for 'peaceful co-existence'
	May	● Warsaw Pact formed
1956	February	● South Vietnam, backed by US, refuses to hold unification elections (as promised at Paris in 1954)
	October	● Hungarian Revolt against Soviet control begins
	November	● Soviet troops invade Hungary
1957	October	● USSR launches Sputnik
1958	January	● Viet Cong set up in South Vietnam
1959	January	● Castro's revolutionary government takes control of Cuba
	December	● NLF set up in South Vietnam, and receives aid from North Vietnam
1961	April	● US-backed Bay of Pigs invasion of Cuba fails
	August	● New crisis over Berlin – the Berlin Wall is built
1962	October	● Cuban Missile Crisis
1963	June	● Hot Line established
	August	● Nuclear Test Ban Treaty
1964	August	● Gulf of Tonkin Incident
1965	March	● First US troops sent to South Vietnam
	July	● 180,000 US troops sent to South Vietnam
1968	January	● Tet Offensive
	April	● Dubcek begins 'Prague Spring' in Czechoslovakia
	August	● Warsaw Pact forces invade Czechoslovakia
	November	● Brezhnev Doctrine
1969	January	● Nixon becomes president of the US – promises to end the war in Vietnam
		● US–USSR relations begin to improve ('Détente')
	June	● 'Vietnamisation' – the first US troops are withdrawn
	November	● My Lai Massacre exposed
1973	January	● Vietnam ceasefire agreed. US troops start to withdraw

1975	March	● North Vietnam launches attack on South Vietnam
	April	● North Vietnamese victory ends war; Vietnam re-united
1979	December	● Soviet troops intervene in Afghanistan
1980	January	● US president Carter imposes a trade embargo on the USSR
1981	January	● Reagan becomes president of the US
1985	March	● Gorbachev elected General Secretary of the CPSU
1989	January	● Soviet troops leave Afghanistan
	June	● East European governments start to collapse
1990	October	● Germany is re-united
1991	December	● Collapse of the USSR; end of the Cold War

Mind Map

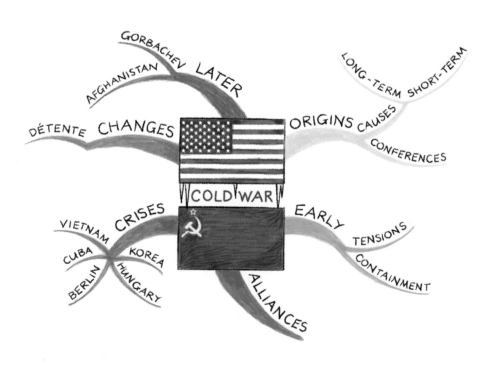

Exam Questions and Students' Answers

1 (a) Explain why the USA introduced the Marshall Plan. [6 marks]

The Marshall Plan – or Marshall Aid – was a form of US aid to the countries of western Europe after the Second World War. This was spread over four years, and was a massive $17 billion. How the aid was to be spent, however, was not to be decided by individual countries. Instead, the Organisation for European Economic Co-operation (OEEC) was set up; the aid could only be used to help develop capitalism. So, the US introduced the Marshall Plan in 1947 to stop the spread of communism at the end of the Second World War – Truman later said that it was the second half of the Truman Doctrine which was about containing (or stopping the spread of) communism.

This was because at the end of the War, the Soviet Union took over the countries of Eastern Europe, such as Poland, Czechoslovakia and Hungary. This is what Churchill in a speech called the 'Iron Curtain'. There was also a civil war in Greece between royalists and communists, and the communist parties in France and Italy were also quite popular immediately after the War because of their part in resistance movements and the role of the USSR in destroying the bulk of Hitler's armies on the Eastern Front. The USA was opposed to communism because it was a capitalist country. The USA was the capitalist superpower (with NATO) and the Soviet Union was the communist superpower (with the Warsaw Pact).

$3/6$

This answer scores three marks because:

► **it clearly identifies one reason** why the USA introduced the Marshall Plan (to stop the spread of communism in western Europe);

► as well as identifying a reason, **some detailed factual knowledge is provided in order to support/explain the reason given.**

To score full marks, you also need to:

► **identify AND explain a variety of different reasons.** These could include:

- the desire of the US to help relieve the terrible economic hardships of the countries of Europe after the Second World War (most countries, including Britain, were so short of food that rationing had to be introduced, while lack of coal, etc., led to electricity cuts and reduced factory production);
- the belief that it would allow the US to export more goods if European economic recovery was speeded up;
- the belief that dependence on US money would allow the USA to be dominant in Europe after the Second World War ('Dollar Diplomacy');
- to 'win' some of the countries of eastern Europe over from the Soviet sphere by offering help which the war-devastated USSR could not provide.

1b

(b) 'The most important cause of the Cold War was the suspicion and rivalry between Truman and Stalin.' Do you agree with this statement? Explain your answer.

[10 marks]

I do not agree with this statement that the most important cause of the Cold War was the suspicion and rivalry between Truman and Stalin. From my own knowledge, I know that the main cause of the Cold War was the same reason I gave in my previous answer about why the USA introduced the Marshall Plan. This was because the USA and the Soviet Union were two superpowers with completely different economic and political systems. The USA was (and still is) capitalist which means they believe that factories, mines, land and banks should be privately owned. But the USSR was communist and believed that all of these things should be owned by the government (nationalised).

Ever since the Bolshevik Revolution in 1917, the US and other western countries had feared Communist Russia because communists wanted a revolution to overthrow capitalism all over the world. During the Russian Civil War between the Reds and the Whites, the western countries had sent armies and supplies to the Whites to help them overthrow the Reds (Communists). Though the communists won, the USSR was left isolated and from then on was afraid that the western countries might try to invade it again. It was only because of Hitler and the Nazis that the USA and the western countries made an alliance with Stalin – up until then, both sides still hated each other.

Even before Germany and Japan were defeated, the old hatred and disagreements between the USA and the USSR had begun to reappear – after the Yalta Conference these disagreements became more serious, for example, at the Potsdam Conference and especially after the USA refused to share nuclear weapons with the Soviet Union. So it was the clash between capitalism and communism which was the main cause of the Cold War. This is why the Cold War ended in 1991 when the communist governments of Eastern Europe and the USSR fell.

4/10

This answer scores four marks because:

► **it identifies AND explains one reason** for the Cold War (the long-term rivalry between two very different economic and political systems, dating back to 1917).

To score full marks, you also need to:

► **consider and fully explain a range of different causes, giving detailed supporting information for each one.** For example, the mutual personal dislike between Truman and Stalin (Stalin had had better relations with Roosevelt); misunderstanding of the other side's motives (the US did not appreciate the full extent of the USSR's human and material losses during the Second World War, or the fear of another invasion across the borders with eastern Europe, while Stalin tended to assume that all suggestions from the USA were designed to keep the USSR weak); and the rivalry for influence in Europe between the two superpowers which emerged at the end of the War.

► **attempt to compare the relative importance of the various possible causes** – i.e. showing how some were more important than others;

► **construct an argument which tries to show how the various causes are all linked together, and that no single cause could fully explain such a complex historical question** – even though some seem to be more important than others.

DON'T MAKE THESE MISTAKES ...

✗ With 'why' questions make sure you **avoid producing an answer which merely identifies one reason – you must try to mention at least two or three reasons.** If you only give one, you will probably only get half marks.

✗ For the highest-scoring questions which ask you to explain and analyse more complex historical issues, again **make sure you consider a wide range of explanations/ factors.** If you only discuss and describe one reason/factor, you will get less than half marks.

✗ Also, you must do more than simply identify a number of reasons – **you must try to give precise supporting details of own knowledge to show how/why these were important reasons.**

✗ If the question gives you a statement and asks you whether you agree with it, **try to produce a balanced answer which shows that there are several different possible reasons/factors, and that no single one is 'the most important' cause** – instead, they are all inter-linked.

Questions to try

Question 1

EXAMINER'S HINTS

✔ With 1(a), which is a why/explanation question, **make sure you do more than simply describe the events – you must try to show why something was important.**

✔ For 1(b), which requires you to use sources to explain different interpretations, **make sure you use the provenance/attribution details provided.**

✔ Try to consider factors such as bias, reliability, propaganda, etc.; and don't forget to use your own knowledge as well.

This question is about superpower involvement in Korea.

(a) Below is a list of important events in the Korean War.

North Koreans cross the 38th Parallel in 1950.
UN forces land at Inchon in 1950.
Chinese forces enter Korea in 1950.
Truman sacks MacArthur in 1951.

These events are in the correct order. Choose any two and explain why each was important.

[4 marks]

For question 1(b) refer to sources A and B.

SOURCE A
Soviet history book, 1984.

The American military intervention in Korea worsened the already tense international relations. The USA was trying to gain control of the whole country. By starting a civil war the South Koreans, supported by the United States, had turned Korea into an international war-zone. Soviet and Chinese help to the People's Democratic Republic of Korea halted the plan to take over North Korea.

SOURCE B
Written by a British journalist who opposed Britain's involvement in the Korean War.

The same complaints made against the government of North Korea can be made against the South Korean government. In South Korea those defending democracy were as vicious as those defending Communism in North Korea. Both sides were guilty of using atrocities to defend their own way of life. So neither the United Nations nor the communist countries could claim to be defending freedom and justice in Korea.

(b) The involvement of the superpowers in the Korean War is open to different interpretations. Do you agree? Using the sources A and B and your own knowledge, give reasons for your answer.

[6 marks]

Question 2

EXAMINER'S HINTS

✔ For 2(a), don't just describe how the views differ – you have to give reasons why they might differ. **You will need to consider factors such as dates, reliability and, especially, motive and purpose.** Also, make sure you use both the sources and your own knowledge.

✔ With 2(b), **try to give a balanced answer which puts the cartoon in the context of the Cold War.**

This question is about the Cuban Crisis of 1962.
Study Sources C, D and E.

SOURCE C
From *The Cuban Missile Crisis: Thirteen Days* by Robert Kennedy, the brother of President John F. Kennedy, published in 1969.

It was estimated that the missiles on Cuba had an atomic warhead power of about half the current missile capacity of the entire Soviet Union. The photographs indicated that missiles were directed at certain American cities. The estimate was that within a few minutes of the missiles being fired 80 million Americans would be dead.

SOURCE D
From *A History of the World in the Twentieth Century* by J. A. S. Grenville, published in Britain in 1994.

In June 1961 President John F. Kennedy met the Soviet leader Nikita Khrushchev in Vienna. Kennedy was not at ease and this led Khrushchev to underestimate him. Khrushchev knew that the Soviet Union was hopelessly inferior in nuclear missile strength and that she was ringed by nuclear bases in Turkey and Western Europe.

During the summer of 1962 Khrushchev decided to move missiles into Cuba. These would act as a deterrent, protect Cuba from invasion and help to even up the balance of power.

President John F. Kennedy felt that there was no more danger to the USA from missiles stationed in Cuba than there was from those stationed 5,000 miles away in the USSR. The problem for him was that if he had done nothing about the Soviet missile bases in Cuba he would have been seen as weak by the people of the USA. He could not afford to suffer another defeat over Cuba.

SOURCE E
A British cartoon drawn in 1962.

(a) Study Sources C and D and use your knowledge. These two sources give different views of the danger to the USA of the missiles on Cuba. Why are these views different? **[10 marks]**

(b) Use Source E and your knowledge to answer this question. Does Source E add to your understanding of the Cuban Missile Crisis? Explain your answer. **[10 marks]**

Question 3 — EXAMINER'S HINTS

✔ Make sure you do more than simply comment about reliability – **you must focus on the use/usefulness of BOTH the sources.**

✔ Also, don't just deal with the content of the sources – **you must include comments about the nature of the sources**, e.g. type/motive/purpose/position of source/author.

This question is about opposition to US involvement in Vietnam.

Study Sources F and G. How useful are these two sources as evidence of opposition in the USA to the country's involvement in the conflict in Vietnam?

[8 marks]

SOURCE F
Extract from *If I Die in a Combat Zone*, a novel by Tim O'Brien written in 1969 and based on his experience as a conscript in Vietnam. Here he describes a conversation he had with an army chaplain.

'Look, what do you know about Communism, O'Brien?' 'Well Sir,' I replied, 'there's little evidence that South Vietnam under the Communists will be a worse place than South Vietnam ruled by the corrupt Diem. I mean there's no evidence that all the lives being lost, the children being napalmed and everything – there's no good evidence that all this horror is worth preventing the North taking over the South. I see evil on both sides.'

SOURCE G
A photograph of a rally in New York's Central Park, in April 1967, held to protest against the war in Vietnam. It was taken by a US press photographer.

The answers can be found on pages **108–112.**

1 The First World War

Question 1

(a) A 'Pals Regiment' was made up of men who lived in the same village or streets, or who worked in the same factory. The army promised to keep such men together in order to get them to volunteer.

(b) DORA was passed to control the Home Front. The main features of DORA were meant to keep up production of weapons and food during the war. The government could take over war-production factories if necessary, and the hours of work were increased. To keep up food supplies – especially after the U-boat attacks – steps were taken to stop waste, and rationing was introduced. DORA also allowed the government to take over land, such as public parks.

DORA also introduced censorship of newspapers so as not to alarm civilians about casualties or give valuable information to the enemy. Under it, people were also told to stop spreading rumours or discussing military matters in public. It was all part of total war.

(c) Conscription was introduced by the British government in 1916 because so many soldiers were being killed in the trenches and fewer people were volunteering. At first, many rushed to volunteer because of patriotism and wanting excitement, and everyone thought it would be over by Christmas. By 1915, about a million men had volunteered.

The heavy losses in battles, such as the battle of Ypres, turned the stalemate of trench warfare into a war of attrition, so huge armies were needed. In January 1916, all single men aged 18 to 40 could be conscripted; then in May 1916 it was also applied to married men. In 1918, because so many more men had been killed, the age was raised to 51.

Another reason conscription was introduced was that the system of volunteering had resulted in many important war industries being short of skilled workers. This was especially true of the important industries of engineering, steel and coal mining. Conscription overcame this by introducing 'reserved occupations' so that key workers could be exempted from service. This meant better planning as regards recruitment, and stopped vital industries being disrupted.

What makes these good answers?

The following points were important in gaining the answers full marks:

► The answer to (a) makes **two brief points of accurate knowledge** and so scores full marks, **without wasting time** on a **low-scoring** question.

► The answer to (b) starts and finishes with **sentences which show a good general/ overall understanding of the purpose** of DORA; it then goes on to describe, as requested, **with accurate detail**, three of the most important features of the Act.

► The answer to (c) answers the question directly – i.e. it **explains why conscription was introduced**, rather than simply writing down facts about how conscription operated. There are also **several good explanations, supported by accurate facts.**

Other possible points to include:

- For (b), your answer could also have mentioned how DORA took steps to prepare for possible invasion.
- For (c), another important reason for conscription was that many people thought that volunteering was an unfair system.

Question 2

These sources do show a lot about the role played by women in the First World War. Source A is useful as it shows that many women did the dangerous work of making shells. By the time the war ended, over 900,000 women were working in such factories – they were called munitionettes. Source B, which was written in 1915, is quite useful as it is true that at the beginning of the war, most women did encourage men to volunteer. This letter was written before the Battle of the Somme, and is probably typical of many women's feelings at that time. Recruitment campaigns encouraged women to use emotional blackmail to get men to volunteer – many gave out 'white feathers' to young men not in uniform. Source C is more useful, as it is about the Voluntary Aid Detachment. Many women volunteered to join this – as the poster shows, many acted as nurses on the various fronts, while others drove ambulances, or were motorbike messengers. But most VAD women did more traditional women's work – the poster mentions many of these, e.g. cooks, kitchen-maids, house-maids and laundresses.

However, the sources don't show all the things women did to help the war effort. For example, many women joined the Women's Land Army – none of the sources mention this. Many women joined to take the place of men at the Front and did the farm work usually done by men. Also, lots of women took over other jobs normally done by men, e.g. bus and tram drivers, ticket inspectors, repairing roads, and working in ordinary factories which were not making things for the war. Nearly 500,000 women acted as clerks and secretaries in offices. By the end of the war, there were over 2 million more women working than there had been in 1914. This was all part of total war. So, overall, the sources do not provide enough information about what women did in the war.

What makes this a good answer?

The following points were important in gaining the answer full marks:

► **All three sources are used, and detailed comments are made** (Source A for munitions work, Source B for women's efforts to encourage men to volunteer, and Source C for the other kinds of war work done by women).

► The answer also brings in **specific extra own knowledge**, e.g. the number of 'munitionettes', the more traditional roles filled by women in the VAD, the numbers of women doing other war work – none of which is mentioned by the sources.

► There is an **attempt at overall balance**, and the final sentence gives a **clear judgement** in response to the question.

Other possible points to include:

- When dealing with the issue of women working in factories, you could mention the fact that, in 1915, the government called for women to volunteer for industry. In that year, Lloyd George (who was Minister for Munitions then) helped to pay for a demonstration organised by Mrs Pankhurst to encourage employers to hire more women to work in munitions factories.

2 The Peace Treaties

This cartoon is trying to say that the Treaty of Versailles will lead to another war. The title of the cartoon shows this, by saying how the peace will result in 'cannon fodder' in the future. It even says when: the child who is weeping over the Peace Treaty is called the '1940 class'. This means that the child (and all other children of the same age) will have to fight another war in 1940.

I know this is about the Treaty of Versailles because it refers to 'The Tiger' – he was Clemenceau, the prime minister of France (it was a nickname). It also shows the others of the Big Three: Lloyd George of Britain and Woodrow Wilson of the US. These were the people who drew up the Treaty. I think the cartoonist is against the Treaty, because it was too harsh on Germany. And he was nearly totally right, because the Second World War started in 1939.

What makes this a good answer?

The following points were important in gaining the answer full marks:

► First of all, there are **several precise references to, and use of information from, the cartoon** – the title, the date over the child, the adults depicted.

► More importantly, the answer doesn't just describe/list points from the cartoon; **historical knowledge is used to explain** the meanings of the points in the cartoon.

► Finally, there is a **clear general/overall judgement** about what the cartoonist is trying to say.

Other possible points to include:

● You could mention that the cartoon is a little unfair on France – Clemenceau only pushed for a harsh peace on Germany when it became clear that the USA would not wipe out France's massive war debts, while Britain refused to agree to a strong League of Nations. In fact, France's Field-Marshal Foch called the Treaty 'an armistice for twenty years', predicting a new war in 1939.
● You could say that the other character in the cartoon is Orlando, the prime minister of Italy (one of the Big Four at the Paris Peace Conferences).

The two cartoons agree and disagree. What they agree on is that there was a problem over the payment of reparations by Germany after the war. The two cartoons were published in 1921 – this was when the Reparations Committee said Germany had to pay £6,600 million. The effect of reparations in Source B (unlimited compensation) is making it impossible for the horse (Germany) to pull the cart; the reparations in Source C are shown as water, which Germany is saying is drowning it ('Help! Help! I drown!'). Both cartoons also show that Lloyd George and Briand were involved in trying to deal with the problem.

Also, the cartoons agree on the role of Briand – in Source B, he is shown as being especially tough on Germany (he is holding a whip and is pulling the reins), and in Source C he is not doing anything to help Germany.

However, though these cartoons are both British, they do not totally agree because they have different views. Source B is showing that the load of reparations really is too big for Germany, but Source C is saying that Germany could pay but is trying to pretend that it can't pay, and so needs help ('loan' is printed on the lifebelt). So, the two sources agree and disagree.

What makes this a good answer?

The following points were important in gaining the answer full marks:

► It begins well by showing the examiner that a **balanced answer** is going to be written: 'The two cartoons agree and disagree.'

► The answer then goes on to **pick out details from both sources** to show how they agree **and** disagree.

► **A little bit of own knowledge** is used to support some of the explanations; and it is clear that **the provenance/attribution details of each source have been used** (e.g. 1921).

► There is a clear **concluding comment** at the end of the answer ('So, the two sources agree and disagree.').

Other possible points to include:

● You could point out that Lloyd George's attitude seems to have changed, even though both cartoons are British and were published in the same year (1921). In Source B, he seems genuinely concerned because he thinks the Allies have put too big a load of reparations on the cart, and wants to help; but in Source C, he is agreeing with Briand in thinking that Germany could pay if it wanted to.

---

3 Weimar and Nazi Germany, 1918–1945

Question 1

The hyper-inflation of 1923 was caused by the French occupation of the Ruhr and the German government's decision to simply print more money. This led to a complete collapse of the German currency and a rapid and huge increase in prices. By November 1923, a loaf of bread cost over 200 billion marks. Because of this, workers were soon paid daily or even twice a day instead of once a week. Middle-class people were not in unions and found it harder to increase their wages, and their savings were wiped out. People on fixed incomes, such as pensioners, were hit especially hard.

However, these great problems led to a new government taking over. At first, this was led by Gustav Stresemann. He began to improve things by introducing a new currency, the Rentenmark. Later, he also got loans from the USA, such as the Dawes Plan in 1924, to help pay reparations and to revive German industry.

But another effect was that many middle-class Germans – especially the conservatives and the extreme nationalists – blamed the Weimar Republic for all their sufferings, and this led to a long-term loss of faith in democracy which Hitler used after the Depression hit Germany in the 1930s.

What makes this a good answer?

The following points were important in gaining the answer full marks:

► The answer gives a **range of effects – both immediate and long term**. The answer refers to what happened to the currency and to prices; the impact on different sections of German society; the actions of Gustav Stresemann; and the general loss of support for the Weimar Republic.

► These examples are then **supported by precise information**: the cost of bread, the name of the new currency and the details and date of the Dawes Plan.

Other possible points to include:

● The Nazi Party's Beer Hall Putsch in Munich in November 1923, which was an immediate response to these problems – although this attempt by Hitler to gain power was unsuccessful.

● The improvements to the German economy during the second half of the 1920s which resulted from Stresemann's policies. These kept the Nazis from electoral success before 1929.

Question 2

There are several reasons why the Nazis did not do well in elections before 1930. One reason was that in November 1923 Hitler tried to overthrow the government by starting a coup in Munich. But this Beer Hall Putsch was a failure; the Nazi Party was banned and Hitler was put in prison. While he was in prison, his party began to break up. This weakened the Nazis and Hitler spent a lot of time from 1925 in trying to reorganise it.

More importantly, by the time Hitler was out of prison German governments – especially because of Stresemann – had done much to revive the German economy. This was mainly because of the Dawes Plan in 1924 and the Young Plan in 1929, which gave Germany large loans from the USA. This meant that most Germans were content and so did not see any need for extremist parties.

Also, the governments had done something to improve Germany's position in Europe. For instance, there was the Locarno Treaty of 1925, and in 1926 Germany was allowed to join the League of Nations. All of this – and the economic improvements – led to a loss of support for far-right parties like the Nazis, as many people were pleased by these things. The Communist Party also saw their support drop.

It wasn't until the death of Stresemann and then the Wall Street Crash in October 1929, which led to high unemployment, that the Nazis began to increase their votes.

What makes this a good answer?

The following points were important in gaining the answer full marks:

► This answer **does more than just list or describe reasons** why the Nazi Party had little political success before 1930. Instead, **the reasons are explained** (e.g. 'This meant that most Germans did not see any need for extremist parties,' and 'All of this...led to a loss of support for far-right parties...').

► The answer **deals with three separate reasons**, not just one or two.

Other possible points to include:

- Specific details of how the Nazis' electoral support declined – in 1924 they had 5% of the seats in the Reichstag; by 1928, this had dropped to less than 2% and the Nazis became the smallest party.

Question 3

Both these sources have their uses, but there are also problems with each of them. Source A is useful because it provides evidence of one of the main functions of the SA (Stormtroopers or Brownshirts), which was to eliminate any political opposition to the Nazis – especially, as in this source, from working-class organisations such as trade unions, and left-wing parties like the SPD and KPD. The photograph indicates the paramilitary nature of the SA, as it shows a heavy machine-gun – the SA often used violence before and after Hitler came to power. Although it is only one photograph and so might be untypical and therefore unreliable, it does actually tie in with what is known about the SA.

Source B also gives information about the activities of the SA – in his speech, Hitler claims that Ernst Röhm was preparing 'violent disturbances' and even a 'revolution'. Although it is true that Röhm and the more militant sections of the SA did want a 'Second Revolution', this source does not really tell us much about the official activities of the SA, so seems to be less useful than Source A.

However, both these sources have their limitations. Source A has no information about who took the photograph, or what it was intended for – it might be a piece of official Nazi propaganda designed to intimidate possible opponents. Source B might also be unreliable, as it is from a speech; politicians do not always tell the truth in speeches to the general public. This is probably true of Source B, as Hitler is trying to justify the actions he took in what became known as the Night of the Long Knives – this was the murder of Röhm and many other leaders of the SA (about 400 in all were killed by the SS). So both these sources are only useful to a certain extent because of these limitations.

What makes this a good answer?

The following points were important in gaining the answer full marks:

▶ It deals with the **content and the provenance information of both the sources.**

▶ It clearly shows the **positive and negative features of both the sources.** Principal Examiners take a lot of time to select sources that have uses and limitations; no source, however unreliable, will be totally useless.

Other possible points to include:

- Even if Source A is a piece of Nazi propaganda, it would be a useful example of this. It might also have been an example of anti-Nazi propaganda, attempting to show the Nazis in a bad, violent light, acting against workers and their organisations.
- It might be helpful to add that Source B was said at a time when Hitler no longer needed the SA as much as he had in the period before 1933. After 1933, Hitler increasingly saw the SA as a threat to his personal power.

Question 4

The main reason the Nazis increased their support in the period 1929 to 1933 was because of the effects of the Depression, which began to hit Germany in 1930 after the Wall Street Crash of the US stock market in October 1929. Up until then, Germany had been quite prosperous for about five years. This was mainly due to the loans from the USA which were provided by the Dawes Plan of 1924 and the Young Plan of 1929. These had helped Germany pay reparations and had revived Germany's factories. As a result, the Nazis had done badly in elections – in 1928, they had only 12 seats in the Reichstag.

However, the Depression ended the loans from the USA and old loans had to be repaid. Factories had to close, and by 1932 there were over 5 million unemployed in Germany. While many workers began to support the Communists, many middle-class people began to desert their traditional parties and vote for the Nazis. This was because Hitler promised to help small farmers and shopkeepers, to reduce rents and interest rates, and to stop the spread of Communism.

The coalition governments which had ruled Weimar Germany since 1918 couldn't agree on what actions to take to solve these problems, and there were several changes of government. This confusion was another reason why many people turned to the Nazis, who promised to bring order and strong government to Germany. This is why the Nazis did so much better in the elections held between 1930 and 1932. In 1930 the Nazis got 107 seats, and in the July 1932 elections they went up to 230 seats and became the largest party in the Reichstag. Hitler also got 13 million votes to von Hindenburg's 19 million in the 1932 presidential elections.

As the Communists also continued to gain more seats, many wealthy industrialists began to give money to the Nazis, which was then used to improve their propaganda and publicity, and to organise huge rallies and campaigns – such as the 'Hitler over Germany' campaign. As a result of all this propaganda, which was organised by Goebbels, and their policies against the Treaty of Versailles, the Weimar Republic and the Communists, the Nazis were able to get more votes. Other reasons for their increased support were their anti-Jewish racism and the violence of the SA. But these were less important.

What makes this a good answer?

► The **focus is clearly on the period specified by the question** – 1929 to 1933. Though there is a little information about events pre-1929 (the Dawes and Young Plans), this is tied into the main part of the question.

► There is **plenty of precise own knowledge**: unemployment figures, the number of seats won by the Nazis in the different elections, and an awareness of various Nazi policies.

► The answer deals with a **range of different explanations**, and so produces a **balanced answer** that clearly identifies some reasons as being more important than others.

Other possible points to include:
● You could mention how Hitler had discussions with the leaders of the Nationalist Party, and other conservative politicians (as well as with the industrialists – which is mentioned in the answer). These were prepared to give the Nazis their support because Hitler promised he would not implement some of the more 'socialist' parts of the Nazi Party programme.
● You could refer to the political deal between Hitler, von Papen and President von Hindenburg. This is relevant, as it made Hitler the new chancellor, even though the November 1932 elections had seen Nazi support drop (with Nazi seats down to 196), while the Communists increased yet again.

4 The Russian Revolution

Question 1

When the Bolsheviks came to power in November 1917, after their November Revolution which had overthrown Kerensky's Provisional Government, they were faced with several problems. The main problems were how to make peace with Germany, how to solve the problem of land reform for the peasants, how to solve the food shortages in towns, and how to set up a strong government for Russia.

One of the Bolsheviks' biggest problems was what to do about Russia's involvement in the First World War. After years of poor supplies, defeats and heavy losses, many Russian soldiers had had enough – this was one of the reasons why the soldiers hadn't helped the Tsar in the March Revolution. Also, many soldiers were deserting, and even killing officers who tried to stop them leaving the trenches. Since April, when Lenin had returned to Russia, the Bolsheviks had been encouraging this, and in the April Theses they had been promising that a Bolshevik government would make peace immediately. However, the Bolsheviks wanted all countries to stop fighting, but the Allies wouldn't agree, and Germany began to make huge demands for Russian lands. This was a big problem for the Bolsheviks because the refusal of the Provisional Government to pull out of the war was one of the main reasons it fell so easily in November.

Land was also a big problem because the peasants wanted more land – under the Tsar, most peasants had no land at all. The Provisional Government had said that this problem would have to wait until after the war. The Bolsheviks knew this was another reason why Kerensky's government had fallen. In fact, before the November Revolution the Bolsheviks had been encouraging the peasants to take land and the April Theses had promised them land. An extra problem for the Bolsheviks was that they wanted the peasants to set up bigger collective farms, but the peasants wanted to have their own private individual farms, which would be less efficient.

Also, the Bolsheviks had promised the factory workers in towns, who were their main supporters, that there would be more food available. But the peasants, who had been conscripted into the army in large numbers, were now putting great efforts into taking over the landlords' lands, and all of this meant that less food was being produced. This was a worry for the Bolsheviks, as they had promised the workers 'Bread', and it was food shortages that had led to the demonstrations which had sparked the March Revolution.

They also had problems with different regions which wanted to break away, while many areas had stopped obeying the central government during the revolutionary upheavals from March to November 1917. This became worse when Civil War broke out in early 1918.

These were all difficult problems but they had to be sorted out, otherwise another revolution might overthrow the Bolsheviks just as they had overthrown Kerensky.

What makes this a good answer?

The following points were important in gaining the answer full marks:

► This answer does exactly what the question asks – instead of just listing or describing the problems, **precise own knowledge is used to explain why these 'factors' were problems.**

► In addition, **this answer gives a variety of problems**, not just one or two. This is important as only one problem – even if explained extremely well, with lots of supporting facts – would limit the answer to about 3 or 4 marks at most.

► The answer begins well by **clearly identifying a number of problems** in the first paragraph. The rest of the answer is well constructed, with a series of paragraphs **dealing with each problem in turn**. The last paragraph then pulls it all together – though this is not necessary to get full marks.

Question 2

I disagree with the statement because, although the defeats in 1914–15 were important, it was the overall impact of the First World War that was more important. Also, there were other reasons why the Tsar fell from power in March 1917. However, it is true that defeats such as at the Battles of Tannenberg and the Masurian Lakes caused great anger, and this led to the Tsar taking personal charge in 1915. But, as Source A says, things did improve after Tannenberg, as regards both better supplies of weapons and ammunition, and morale – 'Now the men are splendid'. One result of this was General Brusilov's offensive in June 1916; this was successful at first, and resulted in the capture of over 250,000 German soldiers. This improved position is supported by Source B, which shows the increased supplies of weapons and ammunition in the period 1915–16, and by Source C, a modern history textbook, which says that 'at the start of 1917 Russia looked strong enough to fight on. . . . They had more men, more guns and more ammunition than the enemy.' In addition, other reasons for the growing numbers of mutinies in the Russian army were bad leadership rather than just defeats (Source A says 'The strategies of the generals are brainless'), and a general lack of supplies. So, overall, I do not agree that the defeats were the main reason for the fall of the Tsar.

More important was the overall effect of three years of total war on the economy, the people and the government of Russia. One effect is referred to in Source D, which comments on discontent in Petrograd being linked to lack of food ('there is no bread'). Source F, which is another history textbook, backs this up when it talks about 'food and fuel shortages due to the war'. The agricultural system crumbled because, by 1916, over 15 million peasants and 60% of Russia's horses had been sent to the Front. The war also caused high inflation, which led many peasants to hoard grain, so causing even greater shortages. Also, much of what was produced was sent to the soldiers at the Front, while the railway system was also disrupted by the war, making it difficult to send what food and fuel there was to the towns and cities of Russia. This was an extra problem because, in order to step up war production, workers in the factories were forced to work longer hours. At the same time their real wages were falling because of inflation (they dropped by 30% in 1917). Many firms went bankrupt because of this inflation, leading to unemployment. As Source F says, these problems were made worse by a particularly bad winter in 1916–17 – 'The first months of 1917 were much colder than usual.' According to this source, some historians argue that it was the weather which sparked off the March (or February) Revolution.

These problems certainly led to an increasing number of strikes and protests. Source D refers to these, while Source E is evidence of a protest in Petrograd in late February 1917. Much of this was largely spontaneous, and revolutionary groups such as the Bolsheviks were not very influential before March 1917. However, discontent had existed before the war. A revolution had broken out in 1905; although this had been crushed and suppressed, by 1912 the number of strikes and protests had begun to increase. In 1914 alone, over 1.3 million Russians took part in strikes. In fact, some historians believe one reason the Tsar entered the First World War was to create a wave of patriotism that would isolate the revolutionaries.

Finally, another factor in the fall of the Tsar was the impact of the war on the government. With the Tsar away at the front after 1915, the Tsarina (who was German) took over – and she was much under the influence of Rasputin. The scandals surrounding him, and the poor decisions he influenced (e.g. the appointment of ministers and officers), did much to weaken support for the monarchy. However, I don't think this was as important as the other factors.

What makes this a good answer?

The following points were important in gaining the answer full marks:

► **Both parts of the question's requirements are met, as the answer links sources and own knowledge throughout.** There are **precise references to all 6 sources**: this is done either by making brief quotes from the sources (C – 'at the start of 1917 Russia looked strong enough to fight on'), or by linking what is in the sources to own knowledge (e.g. B and C are linked to knowledge about Brusilov's June Offensive in 1916).

► There are **several detailed pieces of own knowledge** (e.g. 15 million peasants and 60% of horses sent to the Front, 30% drop in real wages).

► The first sentence states clearly that the writer doesn't agree with the view given in the question, and the answer then goes on to give **a balanced explanation** for this. The answer begins by giving several points to support and oppose the view. Then several other explanations are given by examining **a range of other factors**.

---

5 Stalin's Russia

Question 1

The source shows that under Stalin there was a massive increase of production in coal, oil and steel, which were three of the most important industries in the Soviet Union, and vital for any modern economy. The increase was especially great for coal which by 1937 stood at 128 million tonnes; although this assumes that the figures given are accurate and reliable, which might not be the case. The source also refers to three dates – 1927, 1932 and 1937 – which would probably be the three different Five-Year Plans which Stalin introduced to modernise the USSR's industry.

However, the source does not tell us how Stalin actually went about increasing production. The main way was to draw up Five-Year Plans; this was done by Gosplan, the State Planning Commission, which worked out targets for increased production for each industry, such as coal or steel. Then, targets were drawn up for each mine or factory and eventually for each individual worker.

The First Five-Year Plan concentrated on heavy industry (especially the ones shown in the source) and began in 1928. This was said to have been so successful that the targets were met in four years. So a Second Five-Year Plan was drawn up: this also tended to concentrate on heavy industry, but it also demanded big increases in electricity and engineering (such as machinery for agriculture). A Third Five-Year Plan followed this one and at first tried to do something about consumer production, but this was ended when Stalin ordered increases in military expenditure after Hitler came to power in Germany.

To make sure the targets were met, Stalin used lots of different ways. Crèches were provided so that women with children could work, and factories set up canteens so workers didn't have to go home for lunch. He also used propaganda: in the 1930s, a lot of publicity was given to a miner called Stakhanov who produced well over his target. He was given a medal as a hero of Socialist Production and other benefits, such as better housing and holidays; but other miners then had their targets increased as a result. Workers who did well were said to be making Russia strong.

Other ways of getting workers to meet or exceed their targets included fining people if they were late for work or didn't work hard enough; if they often broke the rules, they could be sacked, deprived of housing or even imprisoned. As a result of all these methods, the USSR soon became the biggest industrial producer after the USA.

What makes this a good answer?

The following points were important in gaining the answer full marks:

▶ The answer is **clearly focused on how fully the source explains how Stalin increased industrial production in the USSR**. It states that despite the information about dates and production figures provided by the source for the period 1927–37, 'the source does not tell us how Stalin actually went about increasing production'.

▶ The answer then goes on to **make good use of own knowledge to show how Stalin did try to increase production**. Not only does it refer to the main method (the Five-Year Plans), but precise details are given: how Gosplan drew up the targets, how there were three Plans in all, and how each of the Plans had a different focus (heavy industry for the First, machinery and electricity for the Second, and consumer goods/light industry for the Third).

▶ As well as dealing with the Five-Year Plans, **the answer is balanced**, in that other **methods are identified** ('crèches', 'canteens', 'propaganda' and 'Stakhanov'), **including more negative ways**, such as being 'fined', 'sacked' or 'imprisoned'.

Other possible points to include:

● A brief mention of how a 'Stakhanovite Movement' was spread throughout the Soviet Union, for all the different main industries.
● You could say more about what happened to people imprisoned for breaking work rules or not meeting targets – many were accused of 'sabotage' and sent to the Gulags (prison work camps), where they were forced to do heavy work with little food, such as building canals, dams, etc.

Question 2

Collectivisation of agriculture was introduced by Stalin for several different reasons. The main one was because he wanted to modernise and expand the Soviet economy by increasing industrial production. This was because he wanted the USSR to be self-sufficient in raw materials and factory goods, and to be able to defend itself from any future attacks. This was why he began the Five-Year Plans in 1928. However, to do this he knew that agriculture would have to be very efficient if it was to feed the increased number of factory workers who would have to leave the land and work in the new factories in the towns.

The problem was that agriculture in the Soviet Union was still very backward. Nothing very much had changed since the revolution of 1917, when the Bolsheviks had allowed the peasants to break up the landlords' land into millions of small private holdings. In particular, very little machinery was used. Although the NEP, introduced by Lenin to replace War Communism, had encouraged the peasants to increase production, it was not able to feed Russia's rapidly expanding factory population – in fact, shortages began to emerge in 1928 and 1929. Stalin and his supporters thought that collectivisation, which would merge many small farms into bigger collective farms, would be more efficient and allow modern machinery to be used to increase food production.

But there were other reasons. As a Communist, Stalin did not like the fact that the richer peasants – the kulaks – sometimes deliberately reduced production, in order to get higher prices for their crops. By 1929, Stalin had come to see the kulaks as a political as well as an economic threat. This was tied in with the last stage of Stalin's political struggle to become the sole leader of the USSR. He had already defeated the Left and now wanted to do the same to the Right, who still supported the NEP and letting peasants keep their own private farms.

What makes this a good answer?

The following points were important in gaining the answer full marks:

► The answer is a **well-balanced** one, in that it **discusses a range of different reasons** – as well as **identifying the more obvious economic ones** (the food crisis of 1928–29, and the desire to modernise agriculture and increase food production). These are clearly put in the historical context (the push to modernise Soviet industry and the Five-Year Plans).

► The answer **also mentions possible political reasons** (the general Communist principle of ending private ownership of land, and Stalin's desire to find a way of defeating his remaining political rivals).

Other possible points to include:

● You could give brief details of the extent of the food crisis – the shortfall in grain production in 1928 was over 2 million tonnes.
● Stalin also wanted to increase food production so he could export food and be able to use the extra money to finance his industrial plans.
● You could give the names of Stalin's different political rivals – Trotsky and Zinoviev for the Left, and Bukharin for the Right.

Question 3

(a) Stalin tried to modernise Russia in several ways. As far as industry was concerned, he tried to expand production by introducing Five-Year Plans, which set targets for each industry. He also used rewards and punishments to make sure people met their targets. In agriculture, he pushed through forced collectivisation in an attempt to increase production, but this was much less successful than his Five-Year Plans – in fact, there was a famine in parts of Russia in the 1930s. He also increased spending on education and health.

(b) Stalin's economic policies were both successful and unsuccessful by 1941. As far as industry was concerned, his Five-Year Plans were quite successful. He wanted to increase production of industries such as coal and steel, and by the end of the

Second Five-Year Plan, a great deal had already been achieved. By 1937, when it ended, coal output was up from 35 million tonnes in 1927 to 128 million tonnes, while steel had gone from 4 million to over 17 million tonnes a year. Big increases in oil, iron and electricity – all important for a modern economy – were also achieved. As a result, the USSR was virtually self-sufficient by the end of the 1930s, had not been affected by the Great Depression, and was second only to the US as a producer of many industrial products. Stalin's policies also meant that the Soviet Union's economy was strong enough to withstand and eventually defeat Nazi Germany, which attacked in 1941. Also, although Stalin often used harsh methods to get these increases, conditions and services did improve slowly for many industrial workers in the 1930s, especially for the skilled.

However, the same cannot be said about his policies for agriculture. The forced collectivisation was hated by the kulaks, who often destroyed their crops, tools and animals rather than see them become part of a collective farm. This, and the mass punishment and removal of millions of peasants, severely disrupted food production, which had already been too low by 1928, before Stalin began his policy. There was also a bad harvest in 1932: as a result, there was a serious famine in some rural parts of the USSR in the years 1932–33. Millions died and the problem was made worse because Stalin ordered grain requisitions to ensure factory workers in the towns had sufficient food. But Stalin was successful in modernising the system of agriculture and getting a greater use of modern machinery and fertilisers; though it is important to note that food production did not begin to recover until 1938.

What makes these good answers?

Question (a)

► There is a **clear focus** on trying to **identify a couple of methods**.

► The answer is **brief** and **doesn't waste time by** going into **detailed** description, which wasn't required. The answer receives top marks without the additional points on education and health.

Question (b)

► The first paragraph starts off well, with an **opening sentence** which flags up that Stalin's policies had **failures** as well as **successes**.

► Both **industry and agriculture** are dealt with, with **plenty of precise own knowledge** to support the points being made – dates and figures relating to the Five-Year Plans, and information relating to opposition to collectivisation and the famine.

► There is an attempt to produce **a balanced answer throughout** – comments about the **negative side of industrialisation, and positive aspects of agricultural policy**, are made.

Other possible points to include:

● You could make comparisons with the slow industrial development under NEP and include information about the new industrial towns, dams and canals built in the 1930s.

● You could mention other negative aspects (e.g. the problems arising from the use of unskilled peasants in factories and how pressures to meet targets often led to shoddy work and falsified figures).

Question 4

(i) Stalin developed the cult of personality to make sure that the Soviet people would remain loyal to him – this would help him stay on as the leader of the USSR. By making it appear that he was always right and the saviour of Russia (almost like a god), the people would worship him as a great leader.

(ii) In the Show Trials, leading Communists who opposed – or who might oppose – Stalin were arrested and put on trial. They were accused of crimes they had not committed (such as sabotage, or being secret agents for capitalist countries) and were forced to admit to these 'crimes' in public trials. This was done by depriving them of sleep, the use of beatings and threats to their families. They were then found 'guilty' and many were imprisoned or even executed. This was done to stop any Communist leaders from even daring to criticise Stalin. Later, even ordinary people were accused in what became known as the Great Purge – all this served to frighten people and so keep Stalin in power.

(iii) Stalin carried out the purges to make sure there would never be anyone capable of opposing his decisions or even overthrowing him. By 1934, the problems with collectivisation were leading some Communists to question Stalin's methods; in particular, Kirov (the Party boss of Leningrad) was popular, and seen by some as a possible successor to Stalin. But in 1934, Kirov was assassinated under mysterious circumstances – some historians think Stalin was behind it.

Stalin then ordered mass arrests and leading Communists such as Zinoviev and Bukharin were sentenced to death after a series of Show Trials. Soon, this led to the Great Purge, in which about 500,000 ordinary Party members were 'purged' – some were executed, while most were sent to the Gulag camps.

This removed the danger of opposition from inside the Party, but Stalin was also afraid that some of the generals of the Red Army might try to remove him – especially in the chaos of a war which, after 1933, when Hitler came to power in Germany, seemed possible. So he began a purge of the officers as well, and about 20% in all were executed or imprisoned.

The purges also affected ordinary people, such as lecturers, teachers, engineers and factory workers. This was done more to frighten the people into supporting him, as these people were not in a position to threaten his position as leader.

(iv) There were several main effects of the purges. Overall, several million people were affected: as a result, people were afraid to point out things that were going wrong in case they were accused of sabotage – this sometimes meant that planning was poor and that materials were wasted, which slowed down the industrial growth of the USSR. But the purges did frighten ordinary people into not opposing Stalin.

Also, the Great Purge badly affected the Red Army, as over 25,000 officers were removed. This meant that when Nazi Germany attacked in 1941, the USSR lacked enough experienced and skilled commanders, and helps explain why the Germans were able to invade so far into the Soviet Union in the first months of the campaign. Because of the purges, therefore, Stalin came close to causing the total defeat of the USSR.

However, the purges did do one thing that Stalin wanted, which was the removal of anyone in the Party or the Red Army who might be a rival and so a threat to his leadership. But in the long term this meant that no-one was confident enough to point out when mistakes were being made. Also, the purges made Communism seem very unattractive and so did nothing to help reduce Russia's isolation in the world.

What makes these good answers?

Question (i)

► The answer has a **clear focus on one reason**, with a **little own knowledge** to explain the point being made about Stalin's desire for total loyalty.

Question (ii)

► This answer gives sufficient **precise information about the trials** regarding the victims (leading Communists) and what happened during them (false accusations, forced 'confessions' in public, and the types of punishments). It then goes on **to show how their scope was widened**, and **links the trials to Stalin's push for control**.

Question (iii)

► This answer is **clearly focused on the demands of the question**, in that it **concentrates on giving reasons for the purges** rather than simply describing the purges – hence it gets the top level, not the bottom one.

► In addition, the answer provides **a range of reasons, not just one**: getting rid of political rivals in the Communist Party; destroying the power of important Red Army leaders; and generally frightening people into supporting him.

► There is also **plenty of precise own knowledge to support the reasons given**: about Kirov and his murder, names of leading Communists, the numbers/ percentages affected.

Question (iv)

► The answer **gives several different effects, not just one or two**: their impact on the Party, the Red Army and people in general; and **attempts to distinguish between short-term** (removing potential rivals from positions of power; consolidating Stalin's control) **and long-term effects** (economic mistakes/ inefficiency; general fear; and the poor performance of the Red Army in the first year of the German invasion).

► There is **some precise own knowledge**: e.g. the number of officers purged; the date of the German invasion.

Other possible/alternative points to include:

● For question (ii), you could give the names of the leading Communists who were victims (Zinoviev, Kamenev, Bukharin, etc.) and the dates of the most famous trials (1936, 1937 and 1938).
● You could include more precise own knowledge (e.g. the names of leading Communists; the fact that the Red Army victims included Tukhachevsky, the Supreme Commander; details of the military disasters and territorial losses in the years 1941–42).
● You could use the terms 'dictatorship' or 'totalitarian' when commenting on how the purges consolidated Stalin's rule.

6 The USA, 1918–1941

(i) Source C does not support the evidence of Sources A and B. Source A says that Hoover was 'unwilling to spend government money to boost the economy'. This is contradicted by Source C, which shows he set up the Reconstruction Finance Corporation in 1932. This was a government agency and made loans to companies to bring 'confidence to America'. However, Source C does support Source A a little, as it says the RFC was 'an emergency measure', so maybe Hoover had changed his mind after he became president in 1929.

Source B, which is from a speech by Hoover in 1930, also shows that he was against government intervention: 'Economic depression cannot be cured by government laws or presidential statements'. But Source C shows that Hoover did actually intervene in 1932 by setting up the RFC. This goes against Source B but, as with Source A, this might be because the Depression had become worse by 1932, two years after he made his speech. So Source C does not really support the other two sources, which both show opposition to government intervention. But maybe he just wanted to give a little help, and then let businesses do the rest.

What makes this a good answer?

► This answer makes **specific and detailed references to all three of the sources** by quoting brief but relevant extracts.

► There is a **clear and balanced attempt to show how the sources both agree and disagree** on the question of Hoover's views on government intervention in the economy. The opening sentence is usually a good way to begin such cross-referencing/comparison questions.

► As well as showing how the sources agree and disagree, there is also an **attempt to explain the differences**; for example, by using the information on dates **(provided by the provenance/attribution details)** to suggest that maybe the situation had become so bad by 1932 that Hoover was forced to change his policy – if only a little.

Other possible points to include:

● A comment about how Source B, like Source A, is also supported a little by Source C could have been made; for example, Source C says Hoover was only willing to let the RFC agency run for two years – this shows he didn't really like the idea of government intervention in the economy.

(ii) There was much opposition to Hoover's policies in the years 1929–33 because he did almost nothing to solve the Great Depression which began in the US following the Wall Street Crash in October 1929. Although many banks and companies went bankrupt, and unemployment rose quickly, Hoover at first did nothing. This was because he was a Republican and so believed in a 'laissez-faire' approach to the economy; this means the government should not interfere in economic and business matters. This is shown in Source A, which says he was unwilling to spend government money and instead believed in non-interference, with the government having the role of 'referee rather than player'. Hoover also believed in 'rugged individualism' which means people should sort out their problems (such as unemployment) on their own. Source B (as well as backing up Source A on the Republican policy of 'laissez-faire') shows this when Hoover says that the problems of the Depression must be solved 'by the producers and consumers themselves'. He was saying this, and that 'prosperity is just around the corner', in 1930 when the Depression had been going for a year – by then, unemployment had already reached 5 million (the figure for 1929 had been 1.5 million).

There were soon many people without food and clothes. The unemployed and homeless were angry that he did nothing to help, so they built shanty towns which they called 'Hoovervilles', and ex-soldiers camped outside the White House to demand early payment of their war pensions – they were called the 'Bonus Army'. But Hoover accused them of being communists and ordered soldiers to break their camp up – this added to his unpopularity. Farmers were also having great problems because of falling prices, which meant many were evicted from their farms because they couldn't keep up their mortgage payments.

Eventually, in 1932, with unemployment at 13 million, Hoover decided to do something. As Source C shows, he set up the RFC to help banks and companies in trouble. However, this was really too little too late; and this then led to many Republicans opposing him as they felt he had betrayed their belief in 'laissez-faire'. Many Americans saw him as a 'do nothing' president and this is mainly why there was so much opposition.

What makes this a good answer?

▶ **This answer does both of the tasks set by the question:** there are **precise references to all three of the sources**; and there are **several items of precise own knowledge** (e.g. 'Hoovervilles', the 'Bonus Army', unemployment statistics).

▶ **Both own knowledge and the sources are used to explain why there was opposition to Hoover** – the answer does more than just describe the opposition (e.g. 'this added to his unpopularity' or 'this is mainly why there was so much opposition').

Other possible points to include:

- Farmers in the Mid-West also suffered from soil erosion (the 'Dust Bowl').
- Hoover also tried to overcome the Depression by making tax cuts in 1930 and 1931, in an attempt to restart the economy. He also urged employers not to cut wages. His belief in 'rugged individualism', however, meant he did not believe in the government providing welfare benefits for the unemployed – instead, he left it to charities which set up soup kitchens and gave hand-outs.

Overall, Statement 1 in Source D does seem to support Statement 2 on the reasons for the introduction of Immigration Laws in the USA in the 1920s. This is because both statements clearly refer to concerns about the numbers of foreign immigrants coming into the USA. Statement 1 refers to 'too many foreigners' coming into America 'without any controls' because of the 'previous "open doors" policy', and Statement 2 also refers to 'new immigrants'. However, the two statements also disagree – Statement 1 gives the 'new mood of isolation after the war' as the reason for the introduction of quotas, while Statement 2 says the quotas were introduced because of fears that the new immigrants 'took jobs away from "real Americans"' and had 'different political ideas which could threaten American democracy'. So, the two statements only agree to a certain extent, which is that quotas were introduced by the Laws to reduce the number of immigrants.

What makes this a good answer?

► **This answer makes specific use of the source** (by quoting brief extracts) to support the points made, so the Examiner can see clearly that the source has been read and understood.

► **A balanced answer has been given**, which shows **both agreement *and* disagreement**; and there is **an overall conclusion/judgement at the end.**

7 International relations, 1918–1939

Question 1

Both of the sources are reliable to some extent as evidence about the actions taken by the League of Nations in response to Italy's invasion of Abyssinia in 1935. Source A suggests that the League – whose main members were Britain and France, shown wagging their fingers at Mussolini – really did nothing serious to try to stop the invasion. The cartoon shows this by saying that, in reality, all Britain and France did was threaten a 'mild disapproval', despite saying they might go to war over the crisis. Although this is a cartoon (which might make it unreliable, as cartoons give one-sided views), it is quite reliable, even though it is criticising Britain and France, as it is from a magazine which normally supported the British government.

Source B is also quite reliable as it is by the British Foreign Minister and he should have inside information about what Britain and the League did about Italy's aggression. More importantly, he said it in 1936, when more facts would have been available, and he said it to a Cabinet meeting. This makes it more reliable because the records of such meetings are kept secret, so he would have less reason not to tell the truth than if he had been talking at a public meeting or to a newspaper. So he feels able to admit that the League's sanctions failed to 'rescue Abyssinia'.

Both these sources also back up what I know about the invasion of Abyssinia. When a crisis first blew up over Abyssinia (because of the Wal-Wal oasis dispute) in December

1934, Britain and France did nothing, even though Mussolini began shipping troops over to Africa. Then the League even suggested that Italy should be given some Abyssinian territory, but Mussolini rejected this and in October 1935 he began a full-scale invasion of Abyssinia. According to the Covenant of the League, sanctions against Italy would have to be imposed immediately. The League set up a committee to decide what these sanctions should be – they decided to ban all arms sales, rubber and metals exports, and loans to Italy, and that all members should ban all imports from Italy. But the most crucial item was oil – the League took till February 1936 to decide to ban it; by then, Italy had got all it needed to complete its conquest of Abyssinia.

Also, the Suez Canal, through which Mussolini transported his military equipment and supplies, was never closed to Italian shipping – even though this was owned by Britain and France. This was because Britain and France didn't want to risk a war with Italy – this is what Source A is suggesting. By May 1936, the emperor of Abyssinia had gone into exile, and the Italians had won and had annexed Abyssinia. So the information in Source B is correct – the way sanctions were imposed was unable to prevent the conquest of Abyssinia. Although both Sources are quite reliable, I think Source B is more reliable because it gives a fuller picture, as Eden (who was speaking in May 1936) will have known the final outcome, whereas Source A was published in 1935 when the problem had only just begun.

What makes this a good answer?

▶ Both parts of the question are dealt with, as **BOTH of the sources are examined AND own knowledge is also used**.

▶ **There are precise references to the sources' content**: 'mild disapproval' from Source A, and the failure to 'rescue Abyssinia' from Source B.

▶ More importantly for a reliability question, **the attribution/provenance information of *both* the sources has been used** to help assess reliability: the fact that Source A usually supported British policy, and that Source B was said at a Cabinet meeting after the invasion had been completed; both the dates given are also used.

▶ **The own knowledge given is precise** – there are references to dates, the League's Covenant, specific details of the various sanctions and the significance of the Suez Canal.

▶ **There is a clear indication of which of the two sources is considered more reliable**, as required by the question.

Other possible points to include:

● Mention could have been made about the lack of close co-operation between Britain and France, as suggested by Source A.
● The reluctance of Britain and France to impose effective sanctions, especially on oil, could have been explained – i.e. that in the circumstances of the Depression, they were afraid of losing trade (especially to non-members such as the USA) and of damaging their own economies (e.g. coal). Also, they did not want to alienate Italy, which was their partner in the Stresa Front (set up after Hitler had tried to take over Austria in 1934) that was intended to block Hitler's plans.

Question 2

I don't think the two sources do provide sufficient information to show why Japan was able to get away with its occupation of Manchuria. However, they do provide some useful facts, especially Source C which is from a history book published in 1954. Historians usually try to be unbiased, and have greater access to documents and other evidence; but despite this, the source really only gives a one-sided explanation. This explanation is that because of the economic depression which had been triggered by the Wall Street Crash in the US in 1929, the rest of the world was so concerned about their own problems that they couldn't be bothered about events in Asia. This is true to a certain extent. It was the effect of the Depression which helped start the Japanese invasion of Manchuria, as Japan was hit badly by the tariffs put on their export goods by countries such as the US and China. However, since the 1920s, the Japanese army had been powerful and was associated with the largest firms which wanted to get the natural resources of Manchuria – an invasion was likely to have come eventually, even without the Depression. It is also true that even important members of the League – including Britain and France – were afraid that imposing sanctions might mean a loss of trade to non-members, such as the US, at a time when their own economies were already suffering.

However, while the Depression was an important factor, it was not the only one. Source D refers to another reason why Japan was able to get away with its invasion. This was the fact that the League did not have its own armed forces, so it could only really impose economic sanctions against a country which used military force. This is shown by Japan having a machine gun, while the League has none and is only able to sentence it to 'a good talking to'.

But there were still other reasons which are not mentioned by either of the sources. These include the slowness of the League in coming to any decision, because of having to have unanimous agreement before anything could be done by the League's Council. When Japan (which was a permanent member of the Council) attacked Manchuria in September 1931, the League's first action was to send the Lytton Committee to investigate the situation. This took months, and by the time the Lytton Committee Report came out in September 1932, Japan had already taken over the whole of Manchuria which was then renamed Manchukuo. Although the League's Council then accepted the Report which said Japan was in the wrong and should return Manchuria to China (which was a League member too), Japan simply ignored it and left the League in February 1933.

There was also another reason why the League did not stop Japan – which is not mentioned by the sources. This was because Britain did not want to risk a war with Japan in Asia, as military leaders told the government that Britain could end up losing important parts of the British Empire, such as India, Hong Kong and Singapore. France was also afraid of a war in Asia – apart from having colonies such as Indochina, France also wanted to keep its army in Europe because Germany was still seen as the main threat. Also, another reason why the League was unable to take action was because two of the world's biggest countries, the US and the USSR, were not members of the League. Although the Soviet Union was concerned by Japan's actions against China, it had no allies and was unwilling to take action alone. The US at this time did not wish to get involved in a war (Isolationism), and even refused to apply economic sanctions against Japan. So this only left Britain and France, and these did not want to take any action.

> ## What makes this a good answer?

► **There are clear/precise references to both of the sources**, which are **clearly focused on the sufficiency of what they say** about Japan's invasion of Manchuria: comments about the effect of the Depression in Source C, and the fact that Japan is shown threatening the League with a machine gun.

► There is also **plenty of own knowledge**, as required by the question – and this is **clearly linked to what the sources do or do not tell us about the events**.

► **The own knowledge is precise and relevant** (i.e. it includes dates, the voting procedures and membership of the League, and how these relate to what the League did or did not do over the attack on Manchuria).

► **It is a balanced answer** – i.e. there are several different reasons given, not just the two provided by the sources.

Other possible points to include:

● Reference to the fact that the cartoon (Source D) mentions the Lytton Report – this is another useful piece of information.
● The fact that France, one of the main members of the League, actually sent a private letter to the Japanese government stating that it 'sympathised' with Japan's 'difficulties' in China. So it is not surprising that the League failed to take action – even though France did vote for action in the Council.
● Mention of the fact that other members of the League – Italy and Germany – held back, as they were interested in seeing if a powerful country could get away with using force in defiance of the League.

8 The Second World War

Question 1

I think Source C does support the evidence of Sources A and B. This is because Source C says that 'the German armies moved forward quickly' and that 'the Poles had little chance', while Source A seems to confirm this where it says 'Gradually the speed increased' and then 'On we went, at a steady speed, towards our objective'. So both these sources are describing the success of the German attack and the failure of the Poles to stop the German Blitzkrieg.

Source C also supports Source B to an extent, as Source C shows the importance of air power in the German attack, where it refers to Stuka dive-bombers finding the Polish troops 'easy targets', and to German tanks. The diagram (Source B) clearly shows how dive-bombers and tanks were important in smashing through the enemy front line and destroying the enemy air force on the ground; it also says bombers attacked towns in order 'to spread panic'.

However, Source C does not fully support Source A, as Source C clearly shows that the Poles did put up resistance – such as making a cavalry charge against German tanks, and crashing their planes into German bombers. But Rommel, in Source A, makes no mention of Polish bravery or opposition. Also, Source C makes it clear that this was not an equal contest, by referring to the Poles being 'outnumbered' and their weapons being 'out of date', whereas Source A makes no mention of Polish weaknesses. In addition, Sources B and C do not necessarily agree totally, as Source B just shows the methods of Blitzkrieg used by the Germans in the Second World War – it doesn't say that the diagram is specifically about Poland. However, I know that this method was used by the Germans at the start of the war, and Poland was one of the first countries attacked by Nazi Germany (which led to Britain and France declaring war on Germany). So, overall, though Source C does support both sources to a certain extent, it gives greater support to Source B.

What makes this a good answer?

► **There are clear cross-references between the correct sources,** C–A and C–B, and a general comment such as 'C agrees with A and B as they are all about the German attack on Poland' has been avoided.

► **There is no attempt to cross-reference A and B** – this would not have gained any marks at all.

► **The cross-references are precise/detailed,** e.g. 'moving forward quickly' in C and 'the speed increased' in A; while own knowledge (about the Blitzkrieg methods and the invasion of Poland) is used to show a connection between C and B.

► Also, **there is an attempt to show that sources A and B are not equally supported by C,** e.g. A makes no mention of Polish resistance or bravery.

Question 2

(i) The figures in Source A do support the view stated at the beginning of Source B, but only to a certain extent. This is because Source A clearly shows that the USA was losing a large number of men in the battles for the Pacific Islands – in just one battle (Luzon, 1945), the US suffered 35,000 casualties. However, Source A also shows that Japan lost many more men, and the US total is nowhere near the million referred to in Source B. Clearly, the greater cost was being paid by defenders rather than attackers. On the other hand, the high number of Japanese casualties shows a determined resistance and perhaps a willingness to fight to the very end – one such desperate tactic was the 'kamikaze' attack.

But Source A is rather limited, as it shows only three battles in the US 'Island Hopping' campaign, and it would be reasonable to assume that Japanese resistance would increase as US forces got nearer to Japan itself. However, US Admiral Nimitz's 'Island Hopping' tactic of concentrating on those Japanese-held Pacific islands which had harbours and airbases meant that, by June 1945, the Japanese had lost control of most of the area. Also, US conventional bombing of Japanese cities was destroying many factories and forcing civilian workers to flee from the cities, thus seriously damaging Japanese war-production. This would have meant Japan would soon have been on the point of surrender, especially as the USSR officially joined the war against Japan after July 1945. In fact, US intelligence services had found out that the Japanese government was ready to discuss peace terms before the atom bombs were dropped. So, overall, Source A only supports Source B to a certain extent.

(ii) There are several different reasons why Sources B and C differ in their interpretation of why the US dropped atomic bombs on Japan in 1945. To begin with, Source B was written in 1945, when all the relevant information might not have been available, whereas Source C was written in 1984, so the writer of this source had the benefit of hindsight and more information. Also, Source B was written by a government official who was present at the time and who 'believed that the atom bomb would be successful' but who, although in a position to know the true reasons, might be trying to justify a decision which came increasingly to be seen as inhuman. The author of Source B tries to equate the decision with the attack on Pearl Harbor, although in this case the target was a military one, as opposed to the mainly civilian cities of Hiroshima and Nagasaki. Source C, on the other hand, was written by a historian who should be expected to give a more balanced explanation.

However, just as Source B was written by someone who might be biased, the same is also possibly true of Source C, which was written by a Soviet historian. As the Cold War, in which the USA and the USSR were opponents, was still going on, it is important to bear in mind that both sides tried to show the other in a bad light. In fact, Source C tries to show how this US action was responsible for the start of the nuclear arms race – this might be why this comment was made. Also, this was written before Gorbachev came to power, so would be liable to official censorship. However, Source C does give the US explanation, even though it then goes on to reject it and instead give an alternative explanation (the start of the Cold War and US attempts to intimidate the USSR by refusing to share nuclear technology with its World War Two ally, the USSR). Similarly, given the date (the start of the Cold War), the writer of Source B might also be trying to deny responsibility for starting the Cold War, and so would be trying to hide the real reasons for dropping atom bombs. The US possession of a nuclear monopoly was not ended until the Soviet Union exploded its first A-bomb in 1949.

What makes these good answers?

Question (i)

▶ **There are clear references to BOTH the sources**, e.g. specific figures from A, 'a million casualties' in B.

▶ As well as using both the sources, **there are also some deductions made from the sources**, e.g. more lost in defending, and Japanese losses suggest they might fight to the end.

▶ **There is also plenty of additional specific own knowledge to add to the information provided by the sources**, e.g. dates, specific references to individuals and tactics, knowledge of other methods (e.g. conventional bombing of Japan, and its effects).

▶ Finally, **limitations of the sources are pointed out**, e.g. A only mentions three battles.

Question (ii)

▶ **There are clear references to both sources**, pointing out the different dates of Sources B and C, and linking these to events/circumstances (e.g. the Cold War, state censorship in the USSR before Gorbachev).

▶ **There are clear attempts to explain the differences** – the candidate has not simply described the differences or merely asserted that they might be biased. Instead, there are attempts to assess the possible influence of the positions/ motives/purposes of the authors.

▶ **There are precise/detailed pieces of own knowledge**, which are added to help explain the differences, by placing the sources in their historical context, e.g. the US nuclear monopoly and its connection to the nuclear arms race.

9 Britain, 1900–1945

(a) Source A shows that suffragists thought women should have the vote because not to let them vote was ridiculous as well as unfair. They thought it was ridiculous because, as the postcard shows, an educated woman (such as a doctor or teacher) had no vote, while all men – even criminals, lunatics and drunkards – could vote. So suffragists thought women should have the vote for practical and sensible reasons, as well as for fairness and equality.

What makes this a good answer?

► **It starts and ends with an overall summary/inference and conclusion** – that suffragists thought women should have the right to vote for reasons of sense, as well as for fairness and equality.

► It also **uses a little of the information provided in the source to support the points made** (women doctors and teachers, though educated, were denied the vote, while men who were criminals, drunkards, etc., had the right to vote).

Another possible point to include:

● The postcard says that denying women the vote was also unfair by showing that, although women did useful and important jobs (e.g. nurse, mother, factory worker), they were still denied the vote.

(b) Sources B and D do support Source C, but only to an extent. Source C is about how the suffragettes were violent and says that 'such things cannot be tolerated'. Source B does support the information in Source C, as it describes what the suffragettes did on the demonstration in London in June 1908. Their actions (such as stone throwing) meant 'violence broke out': this supports the comments in Source C that the 'militant suffragists' 'encourage disorder and riot'. However, Source B does not support the comments in Source C that the suffragettes should be 'punished with the utmost severity'; Source B only describes the actions and feelings of the suffragettes, and doesn't make any judgements about their actions.

Source D also only supports Source C in some aspects. The map (Source D) shows about ten places in Britain where arson was carried out by suffragettes, as well as about four where explosives were used. However, Source D also shows that many of their protests were peaceful: Source C says nothing about peaceful protests. Also, like Source B, Source D does not express an opinion on whether the suffragettes should be punished.

What makes this a good answer?

► **There are clear cross-references between C and *both* B and D:** stone throwing in B, arson and explosions in D, and disorder and riot in C.

► **The answer also shows how B and D *differ* a little from Source C:** Sources B and D make no comment on whether the suffragettes should be punished, they just give facts, and Source D also shows peaceful protests, unlike Source C.

Another possible point to include:

● A concluding comment could have been made that, although Sources B and D do show that the suffragettes' actions were sometimes violent, they do not share the views in Source C on how they should be dealt with.

(c) There are many reasons why women did not get the vote before 1914. As Christabel Pankhurst shows in Source E, the women's suffrage movement was divided; this was because the NUWSS Suffragists were opposed to the more militant campaigns of the WSPU Suffragettes, one of which is described in Source B: the WSPU motto was 'Deeds not Words'. As a result, there was often little cooperation between the NUWSS and the WSPU. As Christabel Pankhurst was one of the main leaders of the WSPU and is therefore criticising herself and her mother and her sister Sylvia, this must have been an important reason. As she says, if the two groups had 'worked together' before 1914, they might have got the House of Commons to 'agree to their demands'.

Another possible reason is that the violent methods of the Suffragettes (WSPU) – such as the arson and explosions listed in Source D – actually prevented them getting the vote earlier. Many Liberals, who were in government from 1906 to 1914, supported votes for women, even some of the leading ministers in the cabinet, but most were not prepared to be seen to give in to violence. For instance, many were angered by Emily Davison's protest at the Derby in 1913, and Liberal ministers, including the prime minister, were furious when Suffragettes disrupted their meetings, chained themselves to railings outside parliament, or caused disturbances in the House of Commons. Lloyd George later said the Liberal government would have 'gladly' given them the vote, but would not back down in the face of the Suffragettes' violence; newspapers such as the one in Source C would have made this difficult. So, when attempts (in 1907, 1908 and 1910) were made by symapthetic MPs to give women the vote, they failed to get through the Commons.

Another reason was that the main political parties were afraid that their opponents might get more votes from women than they would. The Liberals believed most women would vote Conservative, while the Conservatives were afraid that they would not win many votes because women would be grateful to the Liberals for passing the reform, so they only wanted wealthy women to get the vote.

What makes this a good answer?

► **There is a lot of specific factual information** (e.g. about WSPU methods, the views of politicians).

► **There are also several references to four of the five sources;** though these are brief, they show good understanding.

Other possible points to include:

● Many women were also opposed to votes for women for the same reasons as many men. As well as not approving of the violence used by the Suffragettes (which made them seem irresponsible and so not worthy of the vote), many women believed that politics was not suitable for women. Even Queen Victoria (who died in 1901) shared this view of the position of women in society. The prevailing view was that a woman's father or husband would vote in her best interests.

● Mention could also have been made of the fact that Christabel Pankhurst's comments were not made until 1950, so perhaps she was telling the truth, as there was less reason to lie or exaggerate.

10 The Cold War

Question 1

(a) <u>North Koreans cross the 38th Parallel in 1950.</u> Korea, which had been invaded by Japan in the Second World War, had been temporarily divided into North (communist) and South (capitalist) in 1945; both states wanted reunification and both were prepared to use force. When North Korea invaded the South in 1950, it shifted Cold War tensions from Europe to Asia and ran the risk of directly involving the two superpowers in a 'hot' war. This is why it was important.

The US had already been worried by the loss of its nuclear weapons monopoly when the USSR exploded its first A-bomb in August 1949, and by the communist victory in China in October 1949. These events had sparked off the McCarthy witch-hunts in early 1950. Truman, who had been responsible for the policy of containment of communism (the Truman Doctrine), believed the invasion of South Korea was more than a civil war between two undemocratic states. He believed in the Domino Theory and quickly sent US forces to the region. All this greatly increased Cold War tensions.

<u>Truman sacks MacArthur in 1951.</u> This was also important because it prevented a possible nuclear war with China. When the US/UN forces had pushed North Korean forces out of the South, Truman had ordered an invasion of the North and US troops had gone right up to the Chinese border. This led the Chinese to send a large army to help the North and the US/UN forces were pushed back in 1951, and communist forces again crossed the 38th Parallel. MacArthur now wanted to invade China, and he and Truman even suggested using nuclear bombs. By March 1951, the North had been pushed back to the original border – but Truman and MacArthur now disagreed: Truman wanted to negotiate with the Chinese, while MacArthur openly called for the total defeat of China. So Truman sacked him and peace talks began in July.

What makes this a good answer?

► **Both responses use detailed factual knowledge** to explain the events chosen and to put them into historical context.

► **Both responses also attempt to show clearly why the chosen events were important** – e.g. how the invasion gave the US a chance to act on the Truman Doctrine and increased Cold War tensions; how the sacking of MacArthur avoided possible nuclear war and allowed peace negotiations to begin.

Other possible points to include:

● The invasion of South Korea was also important because it allowed Truman to implement NSC 68. This not only turned the Korean dispute into an international conflict (16 countries fought in Korea), but also paved the way for later US involvement in Vietnam.

(b) I agree that the involvement of the superpowers in the Korean War is open to different interpretations. This is because it was part of the Cold War, and some explanations are biased. For instance, Source A (which is from a Russian history book) says the South started the war and that the USSR and China only got involved to help the North. But in fact it was the North who began the war; and the USSR and China knew of the North's plan to invade, and even helped in the planning. So the writer of Source A may be trying to avoid blame for the USSR; and we know that nothing critical of the USSR would have been published at that time in the Soviet Union.

However, the South was also planning to invade the North, and US claims to be supporting freedom were not true as the South was also a dictatorship. Its ruler, Syngman Rhee, was unpopular and many in the South were in favour of unification with the communist North. Source B agrees with this and seems to be reliable (even though the writer is British) as it criticises both sides; though we do not know his personal beliefs. Also, the US did not stop when its forces reached the border in October 1950; instead they invaded the North and at one point even considered invading China. So the USA seemed to be as expansionist as the communists, and appeared to be willing to go beyond the Truman Doctrine's idea of containment to an attempt to 'roll back' communism, as set out in the document NSC 68. But the US and its supporters in the Cold War always portrayed their actions as being support for 'freedom'.

What makes this a good answer?

► **The answer is focused on explaining why there are different interpretations, and there are clear references to the provenance/attribution details of both the sources** to support this.

► **The content of both sources is also considered and is assessed in the light of specific own knowledge.**

Other possible points to include:

● Soviet and Chinese motives for involvement in Korea could have been given – e.g. both these states were worried that an 'unfriendly' government of the whole of Korea might be a threat to their borders and security.

(a) The views are different because they were written by different people, for different reasons and at different times. Source C was written by Kennedy's brother who was also a leading member of the US government and was involved in the Cuban Crisis. By the time it was published in 1969, Kennedy had been assassinated so his brother would not want to say that the risk of a nuclear war had been unnecessary, or to discredit himself and the US government. So, as the US was now involved in the Vietnam War (which many Americans were opposing), this was probably written to show the US public that the USSR really was a threat to US security. During the Cold War, the policy was to build up fear of the 'enemy' amongst the general public. Therefore, although Robert Kennedy was in a position to know the facts of the Cuban Crisis, this source is probably biased and unreliable.

Source D, on the other hand, was published in 1994 – by then, the USSR had collapsed and the Cold War was over, so there was less need to keep the true facts hidden. Partly this is because both the Kennedy brothers were dead by 1994, so there was no need to worry about upsetting anyone. With the Cold War over – and especially in Britain, which was not involved in the Crisis – there was no reason not to tell the truth.

What makes this a good answer?

► **A number of different factors are examined in order to explain the different views** – e.g. the dates of the sources; the 'position to know' of Source C, possible reliability problems with that source, and the possible motives/purpose of Source D.

► In addition, **some detailed own knowledge is also used to help explain the differences** – e.g. the Cold War still being in full swing in 1969 but being over by 1994.

Other possible points to include:

● It was John F. Kennedy's brother who helped end the Crisis by making a secret agreement with the Soviet ambassador to remove US missiles from Turkey if Khrushchev would publicly back down over the missiles in Cuba.

● By 1994, many more documents had become public, so a fuller picture of the events was possible.

● Source D was written by a historian who had access to a wide range of sources and would be attempting to give the full picture, whereas Source C was only giving the US view.

(b) Overall, I think that the cartoon does add something to my understanding of the Cuban Crisis, even though it does not give as much information as some of the other sources. The cartoon refers to several aspects of the Cold War and the Cuban Crisis. For instance, it shows how close the world came to a nuclear war – Kennedy's finger is just above the button that would send off the US missiles which were targeted on Soviet cities. Some Soviet generals, meanwhile, were trying to get Khrushchev to launch missiles rather than back down over the illegal blockade that Kennedy had imposed on ships going to Cuba, while Castro urged the same in order to prevent another US attempt to invade Cuba.

The cartoon also shows Kennedy being calm, as if he knew the US would win; but Khrushchev is shown to be sweating – he is probably nervous because he knows the US has many more missiles than the USSR, and many of them are close to the Soviet Union. So the cartoon shows the unequal balance of nuclear weapons, and the fact that the US were not really worried by the missiles in Cuba but were only trying to get Khrushchev to back down in order to make up for Kennedy's poor performance at the Vienna Conference in June 1961. For Kennedy and Khrushchev, this was just another power struggle between Cold War rivals.

The cartoon also tells us that the nuclear bombs which would have been fired were H-bombs, which were much more powerful than the bombs dropped on Hiroshima and Nagasaki in 1945 – this was why so many people in 1962 were afraid that a thermo-nuclear holocaust might happen.

What makes this a good answer?

► **Several precise aspects of the cartoon are referred to and commented on** – e.g. the sweat on Khrushchev, Kennedy's apparent calm, the 'finger over the button' and the letter 'H' on the missiles.

► **Some detailed factual information is given to explain/add to the various aspects of the cartoon.**

► **The answer is balanced** as it also points out that the source does not provide as much information as the others.

Other possible points to include:

● The Crisis was evidence of 'brinkmanship' – this meant that at times both sides had been prepared to risk a war in order to obtain an advantage. The fear over the Cuban Crisis, however, led to attempts to ease tensions.

Question 3

Source F is quite useful as evidence about US opposition to the involvement of the USA in the Vietnam War, as it gives the attitudes of someone who had been a soldier in the conflict. He clearly sees little point to the war when he says that there's no real evidence to show that 'South Vietnam under the Communists will be a worse place than South Vietnam ruled by the corrupt Diem'. As Diem was the ruler backed by the US in their attempt to prevent the spread of Communism (the 'Domino Theory'), this clearly shows lack of support from this soldier. However, there are also possible limitations to this source: firstly, this is only the opinion of one soldier, so might not be typical; secondly, these views were expressed in a novel and might not be as reliable as a history textbook, which would have examined the attitudes of many more people and would have given a more balanced view. However, from my studies I know that these views were shared by many US soldiers – it was partly this which undermined their morale.

Source G is also useful to a certain extent, as it provides evidence of a protest meeting. This was typical of many such demonstrations which took place in the US during the late 1960s and early 1970s, especially after the 1968 Tet Offensive by the Viet Cong and the North Vietnamese. In fact, at Kent State University four protesting students were shot dead by National Guardsmen in 1970. It is also useful as it shows both black and white Americans were against the war. Reasons for such protests were the huge cost ($28 billion a year) and the growing US casualties (over 300 US soldiers were being killed every day by 1969). Another reason for the protests was US citizens seeing on TV the real effects of their army's tactics on Vietnamese civilians. However, a possible problem with this source is that it might be an example of anti-war propaganda, which was run by some papers in the 1960s. Certainly, the photo shows almost as many photographers as protestors, and most of the latter seem to be young students. But, even if it was set up to look like more people were against the war than really were, it would still be a useful example of such propaganda. Taken together, these two sources are quite useful – one shows opposition within the US army, while the other shows opposition among US citizens.

What makes this a good answer?

► **Both the sources are dealt with** and the **focus is clearly on their use/ usefulness**.

► As well as examining **the content of the sources, the answer also deals with their** *nature*.

► There is an attempt to **show how the sources are both useful and not so useful**; and **some own knowledge** is provided to back some of the comments.